HELL'S *Belles*

HELL'S Belles

A Tribute to the Spitfires, Bad Seeds & Steel Magnolias of the New and Old South

Seale Ballenger

CONARI PRESS
Berkeley, California

Conari Press books are distributed by Publishers Group West.

We gratefully acknowledge permission to reprint the following:
Excerpt from "In Defense of Southern Womanhood," by Julia Reed, *The Oxford American*, Spring 1996. Reprinted by permission of *The Oxford American*. Excerpt from "Following Her Bliss," by Darcy Rice, *Orange Coast Magazine*, December 1995. Reprinted by permission of *Orange Coast Magazine* and Darcy Rice. Excerpts from *Wild Women: Crusaders, Curmudgeons and Completely Corsetless Ladies in the Otherwise Virtuous Victorian Era* by Autumn Stephens. Copyright © 1992 by Autumn Stephens. Reprinted by permission of Conari Press. Excerpts from *Wild Women in the White House: The Formidable Females Behind the Throne, On the Phone, and (Sometimes) Under the Bed* by Autumn Stephens. Copyright © 1996 by Autumn Stephens. Reprinted by permission of Conari Press. Excerpts from *Wild Women in the Kitchen: 101 Rambunctious Recipes & 99 Tasty Tales* by the Wild Women Association. Copyright © 1996 by the Wild Women Association. Reprinted by permission of Conari Press.

The photos and illustrations herein are reprinted by gracious permission of Archive Photo, with the exception of the following, which are used courtesy of Corbis-Bettman: pp.106, 149, 150, 160, 173, 191.

Art direction: Ame Beanland
Cover design and illustration: Suzanne Albertson
Cover photo: Archive Photo
Handtinting of cover photo: Peggy Lindt, Point Blank Design, Santa Barbara, CA
Interior design and composition: Jennifer Brontsema

ISBN: 1-57324-096-6

Library of Congress Cataloging-in-Publication Data
Ballenger, Seale, 1964–
    Hell's belles : a tribute to the spitfires, bad seeds & steel magnolias of the New and Old South / Seale Ballenger.
        p.   cm.
    Includes bibliographical references (pp. 260–262) and index.
    ISBN 1-57324-096-6 (trade paper)
    1. Women—Southern States—Biography.   2. Women—Southern States—History.   I. Title
HQ1438.S63B35   1997
305.4'092'275—dc21   97-14776

Printed in the United States of America on recycled paper.
First printing: August 1997
10 9 8 7 6 5 4

For my mother, Miss Jodie, the original Jezebel in white,
who was, along with the Ladies Aid Society, the inspiration for this book.
And for my father, Jonny, whose prophecy that the South is being taken over
by broken glass, telephone poles, and kudzu seems to be coming true.

CONTENTS

Of Spitfires, Bad Seeds and Steel Magnolias

66As lovely a woman as I have ever seen, bred and nurtured like a gardenia, [my mother] has always seemed somehow odorless and sexless to me, yet viscerally seductive in the manner of Southern women, that taloned species who speak with restrained and self-effacing drawls, fill a room with elegance and vulnerability, move with the grace of wind-tilted cane, and rule their families with a secret pact of steel. The sweetness of Southern women often conceals the deadliness of snakes. It has helped them survive the impervious tyranny of Southern men more comfortable with a myth than a flesh and blood woman.99

—*Pat Conroy in* The Lords of Discipline

Whenever you mention the South, images of plantation homes, cotton fields, and women in hoop skirts spring instantly to mind. Whether wily Scarlett O'Haras in flirty finery or deeply shaken Blanche Duboises teetering enraged on the drunken edge, historically women of the South have been portrayed as exaggerated versions of these two characters thanks to vivid and lasting movie portrayals, both, ironically, played by British actress Vivien Leigh.

First there's Scarlett, who, with grit and determination, resolves that she will "never be hungry again," exemplifying in her struggle the whole of southern resolve. Later the frail Blanche (whose name translated means "white wood") is seen as the ghost of the once vivacious, now war-ravaged Scarlett, fighting to maintain her fierce independence and conniving coquetry, and to hang on to the charm of a legendary world "gone with the wind." Both women are torn apart by outside interlopers (read Yankees) who would force them to face the harsh and cruel realities of life, while Blanche's inability to separate life from illusion ultimately sends her spiraling toward insanity, forever cementing the character of the flighty, shallow, and unstable southern woman in modern folklore.

As a result of these characterizations, the stereotype of the southern belle has evolved into an inflated distortion of these two characters, all but ignoring the major role that African American women have played in southern history. Still perceived as a beautiful demure caucasian creature, the southern female is typically portrayed in the media as using her "feminine wiles" to capture a man "at any cost" in a psychological game of cat and mouse.

Originating from an area of the country prone to legend and exaggeration, the mythology of life below the Mason-Dixon line holds nationwide fascination. Reality, however, paints a far more fascinating picture of the daughters of the Confederacy. Though seemingly patriarchal in perception, the southern female actually serves as the backbone of society: strong and independent, she knows how to rule the roost through indirection and nuance, defining the expression, "the iron fist in the velvet glove." It's a balancing act of toughness and tenderness; the trick is to get what you want without looking like you are even trying. One southern woman, commenting on her sisterhood on the Internet, exclaimed, "The women from the south are a rare and amazing breed . . . we can be delicate as a rose or as tough as an old rawhide bone. We were taught by our wonderful southern mothers exactly how to walk, talk, and dress as southern ladies, but yet know how to get down to the nitty gritty and fish, hunt, and mud ride along with any good ol' southern boy." The women of the South are driven by a uniquely southern take on life and a strength of character molded by their roots.

And southern men are some of their biggest fans. When asked his favorite things about the South, one male writer proclaimed in an Internet chat room: "The women. Why? They know when to send a thank-you note; they're not afraid to stand up and give their 'testimony' during evening worship; good cooking is in their blood; they not only know the rules of college football—they enjoy the game as much as we men do; they're delicate enough to appreciate the finest china but earthy enough to put their hands to a tiller in the garden. They're awesome. God has blessed me by putting me amongst them."

From Mama to Mammy, from Scarlett to Blanche, *Hell's Belles*—often exclaimed in mock piety and defining generations of southern women—is an exuberant and loving celebration of the famous and infamous females of ol' Dixie. Historically stereotyped as well-mannered ladies perfect in manner and appearance, this diverse collection of 200 fascinating individuals includes Caucasians, African Americans, Creole, Native American and Latina women, rich and poor. They all have made their marks upon the world in one way or another, some were shaped by and evoke the manners and habits of old, while others strode boldly out of the past, eschewing stereotypes and convention, out of the South and into the world. From West Virginia to Texas, from southern aristocracy and antebellum homes to the poverty stricken tract houses and trailer parks that often dot the landscape, there's something for everyone—and everything, but the kitchen sink!

1.

Belles–Lettres: Literary and Fictional Belles

There's something about the South that breeds great writers—particularly great women writers. Perhaps it is the grand tradition of storytelling, folklore, and mythology, that has inspired this legacy, or perhaps it is the years of hardship and misfortune that pushed many a belle to forge a bond with pen and paper to create great literature. Whatever the reason, we are blessed with a rich literary tradition, culturally bound and owing a great deal to its origins rooted below the Mason-Dixon line.

Literature's Odd Bird

℀ertainly one of the best of the master southern writers was **Flannery O'Connor,** born in Georgia in 1925. Her stories are all powerfully crafted, and, to the vast majority of her readers, incredibly weird. For example, Hazel Motes, backwoods protagonist of her first novel *Wise Blood*, was such an ardent Christian that he founded the Church of Jesus Christ without Christ and blinded himself so he could see.

Gifted with an extraordinary ear for language and an ability to evoke an almost-tactile experience of the scenes she describes, Flannery O'Connor was also the odd woman out. Largely uninterested in the massive social upheaval of her time (the Civil Rights Movement) and a devout Roman Catholic in the heart of the Fundamentalist South, she wrote stories that all—in one way or another—centered around the profoundly spiritual issue of redemption. But redemption was not a simple concept for her; it was a deeply individual evolution. And to the shock of many a good Christian, her work was populated with the bizarre, the grotesque, the maimed, and the seriously disturbed—and Flannery managed to imbue them all with a powerful, if twisted, sense of dignity. In a way, she was the true chronicler of the underside of southern life; and she used her characters' physical, moral, and mental disabilities to mirror their spiritual struggles.

The most formative event of her childhood was the slow, agonizing death of her father when she was just twelve. He died of lupus—the same disease that would soon take over her own life. After graduating from the Georgia College for Women, she decamped to the Iowa Writers' Workshop where she won the Rinehart-Iowa prize for the beginnings of *Wise Blood*. The award also gave the publisher Holt-Rinehart an option on her novel, which led to one great literary story in hindsight. When Flannery turned in the early portions of *Wise Blood* to the Holt editor assigned to her, he found the manuscript "bizarre" and sent a letter offering to work with her to "change the direction" of her work into a more conventional form. Then only twenty-three years old, she politely refused and pulled the book from Holt, the editor complaining that she suffered from "hardening of the arteries of cooperative sense."

Flannery's vision and style was intensely personal, and though often criticized and generally misunderstood, she never wavered. She once reflected that "I have found . . . that my subject in fiction is the action of grace in territory held largely by the devil. I have also found that what I write is read by an audience which puts little stock either in grace or the devil."

After she too was diagnosed with lupus in 1950, at the age of twenty-five, she moved in with her mother on a dairy farm in north Georgia called Andalusia. By this time lupus was controllable with massive doses of steroids; but it was a debilitating and exhausting existence. Flannery's deep religious beliefs served her well. She graciously accepted her condition and focused all the energy she had on three hours of writing each morning, and raising peacocks.

When she died at age thirty-nine in 1964, she left behind a modest body of work including the novels *Wise Blood* (1955), and *The Violent Bear it Away* (1960), and collections of stories, *A Good Man is Hard to Find* (1955), and *Everything That Rises Must Converge* (1965, published posthumously). But the impact of her words was never measured in quantity. She died recognized throughout the world as a complete original and one of the truly great contemporary American writers.

❝I divide people into two classes: the Irksome and the Non-Irksome without regard to sex. Yes and there are the Medium Irksome and the Rare Irksome.❞
    —Flannery O'Connor

THE LONG ROAD TO FREEDOM

The scope of **Harriet Ann Jacobs'** life runs like a thick cord through the darkest back roads of American history. Her account of her life as a slave and a fugitive is considered by many to be the most complete and compelling first-hand picture of the reality of slavery in the American South.

Born of slave parents in North Carolina in 1813, her mother died when she was six and she was moved into the "big house," where she quickly became a favorite of the mistress, Margaret Horniblow, who taught her to read and write. When she was twelve, Margaret died and instead of being freed as had been promised, Harriet was passed along in the will (along with a set of drawers and a work table) to Margaret's niece.

The niece's father, Dr. Norcom, began to pressure Harriet to become his bed partner. Hoping to put off his intentions, she became involved with the white lawyer living next door and eventually bore him two children. Undeterred, Norcom finally gave her an ultimatum—either become his whore or he'd send her back to work on one of his plantations. Alarmed and fearful that her children would be sent with her, she escaped, hoping that with her missing Norcom would agree to sell her and her children to their father.

Her plan only partly worked. The lawyer did buy the children and sent them to live with Harriet's grandmother, who had won her freedom and ran a bakery in the town of Edenten, North Carolina. Harriet hid in the area for the next seven years, much of that time stuck in a small crawl space seven feet wide, nine feet long, and barely three feet tall. In 1842, she finally managed to make her way north, where she was eventually reunited with her children. By 1849, she had become an abolitionist activist in Rochester, New York, with Frederick Douglas. On a visit to New York City, she was nearly captured off the streets of Manhattan by her North Carolina owner and fled to

Massachusetts. A friend, Cornelia Willis, then bought Harriet's freedom and that of her two children (conducting the purchase without Harriet's knowledge).

The transaction caused Harriet considerable difficulty—she was elated to be truly free and able to live openly without fear, but at the same time felt tainted at having somehow participated in the system of slavery by allowing herself to be bought. Encouraged by friends she had confided in, Harriet set out to tell her story. The result was a self-published book (no one was willing to publish it for her) under the pseudonym of Linda Brent called *Incidents in the Life of a Slave Girl: Written by Herself*. Harriet's authorship of the book was lost to history for many years—it was widely assumed the book had been written as a novel by a white woman—until the real authorship was verified in the late 1980's.

Shortly after her book came out, the Civil War began and Harriet threw herself into organizing relief, education, and basic health care for the growing crowds of slaves fleeing to safety behind the northern lines. Working with her daughter, Louisa, she founded the Jacobs Free School to educate the children of freed slaves and regularly reported the status of relief efforts in the South to the Northern press. In 1868, after moving to Savannah to continue their relief work, Louisa joined with Susan B. Anthony in the effort to get voting rights for women and African Americans written into the New York constitution. In 1869, Harriet attended the organizing meeting of the National Association of Colored Women in Washington, D.C. The following year, she died at the age of eighty-four.

Two or Three Things She Knows for Sure

Born in 1949 in Greenville, South Carolina, writer **Dorothy Allison** first made a name for herself as a poet with *The Women Who Hate Me* (1983), a powerful collection of poems exploring her love and desire for other women. Highlighted by themes involving sadomasochism, promiscuity, and role playing, Dorothy was placed immediately at odds with several feminists of the time for her exploration of boundless sexual freedom. As she said in an interview with the *Advocate*, "I felt like a spy. During the daytime I was a nice, lean, lesbian-feminist living in a collective; at night I was a subterranean slut."

As a child, Dorothy grew up in a harsh world, where the men were abusive and the once beautiful, work-hardened women in the family were the glue that kept everything together. In her 1995 memoir, *Two or Three Things I Know For Sure*, she recounts her southern childhood in aching detail. "Let me tell you about what I have never been allowed to be. Beautiful and female. Sexed and sexual. I was born trash in a land where the people all believe themselves natural aristocrats. Ask any white Southerner. They'll take you back two generations, say, 'Yeah, we had a plantation.' The hell we did."

Moving to fiction in her 1988 collection of short stories, *Trash*—winner of a Lambda Literary award—Dorothy drew heavily on her childhood experiences among the working class poor and the socially despised of the South. In its introduction she writes, "I put on the page a third look at what I've seen in my life—the condensed and reinvented experience of a cross-eyed working-class lesbian, addicted to violence, language, and hope, who has made the decision to live, is determined to live, on the page and on the street, for me and mine."

In 1992, Dorothy published her first novel, *Bastard Out of Carolina*. It is a brilliant story of a young girl, born out of wedlock and into poverty, who—in circumstances nearly identical to the author's own childhood—is subjected to both domestic and personal sexual violence. It garnered significant national acclaim, including a National Book Award nomination for best fiction, and thrust Allison into the glaring media spotlight of the mainstream. Controversial for its no-holds-barred depiction of violence and "how it is intrinsic to family and personal identity," the story of Bone Boatwright left many people shaken, but deeply moved by its raw, sensitive, and unsentimental depiction of tragic circumstances.

Refusing the label of "victim," Dorothy's gift as a phenomenal writer of great emotional power and strength lies in her use of realism and her clear avoidance of exploitation. Though a seeming contradiction, she is the epitome of the strong southern woman, pulled up by her own bootstraps, and motivated by circumstances that have pushed her to greatness.

Dorothy, thankfully, continues to write. She, and her partner, Alix, live in the San Francisco Bay Area, and are the proud parents of a son, Wolf.

66 My sister learned the worth of beauty. She dropped out of high school and fell in love with a boy who got a bunch of friends to swear the baby she was carrying could just as easily have been theirs as his. By eighteen she was no longer beautiful, she was ashamed: staying up nights with her bastard son, living in my stepfather's house, a dispatcher for a rug company, unable to afford her own place, desperate to give her love to the first man who would treat her gently. **99**

  —Dorothy Allison

Wild "Womanist"

$\mathcal{W}$hile she currently lives in California, Pulitzer Prize-winning author **Alice Walker** has never forgotten her rural Georgian roots. "You look at old photographs of southern blacks and you see it—a fearlessness, a real determination and proof of a moral center that is absolutely bedrock to the land," she once said. Certainly that strength, particularly in southern black women, is brilliantly displayed in her most famous novel, *The*

Color Purple, which also draws on her memories of southern landscape and language.

She was born in 1944, the eighth child of poor sharecroppers in Eatonton, Georgia. Her mother encouraged her writing, even going so far as to buy her a typewriter, although she herself made less than twenty dollars a week. In 1967, after college in the North, she married a white man and the duo lived in Mississippi as the first legally married interracial couple in the state. Her marriage, she claims, had a negative effect on her career because it angered black reviewers who ignored her earlier works, including *In Love and Trouble* and *Meridian*. It was her third novel, *The Color Purple*, which rocketed her to fame in 1983 (winning both the Pulitzer Prize and the American Book Award) and embroiled her in controversy, particularly with the male African American community, which claimed the work reinforced stereotypes about black men. The subsequent movie by Steven Spielberg in 1985 only fanned the flames of the imbroglio.

The literary heir of Zora Neale Hurston and Flannery O'Connor, the prolific "womanist," as she calls herself, has penned novels, short stories, poetry, and essays—seventeen volumes in all so far. Each reveals her deep commitment to social justice, feminism, and, particularly, African American women, as seen through her unique, inner vision, a vision she began to develop, she has said, after she became blind in one eye when one of her brothers shot her with a B.B. gun. Forcing her inward, she began to carefully observe the people around her. By writing, she has noted, "I'm really paying homage to the people I love, the people who are thought to be dumb and backward but who taught me to see beauty."

She believes strongly in the power of art to help change the world and the artist's responsibility to that power—ideas she expressed in her collection of essays, *In My Mother's Garden*. In an audiotape entitled *My Life as Myself*, she spoke of her activism: "My way of fighting back is to understand [injustice] and then to create a work that expresses what I understand."

66 I think there is hope in the South, not in the North. **99**
    —Alice Walker

The Grand Dame of Southern Letters

*E*udora **Welty** is known around the world for her compressed, precise portraits of people inhabiting a small Mississippi town that is suspiciously like her own hometown of Jackson and the surrounding Mississippi Delta country. "Southern writers feel passionately about Place. Not simply in the historical or philosophical connotation of the word, but in the sensory thing, the experienced world of sight and sound and smell, in its earth and water and sky and in its seasons."

Eudora's main theme throughout three novels and many volumes of short stories involves the intricacy of relationships between Southerners in the midst of change and is enlivened by her sharp eye, her uncanny ear for the cadences of southern dialect, and a rich, lively sense of humor. Among her best-known works are the hysterically funny short story, "Why I Live at the P.O.," and *The Optimist's Daughter*, for which she won the Pulitzer Prize in 1972.

Born in 1909 into what she would later call "a sheltered life," Eudora was a voracious reader as a child, calling an essay she wrote about her childhood love of books, "A Sweet Devouring." And, like so many Southerners before and since, her life was filled with stories: "All the years we lived in that house where we children were born, the same people lived in the other houses on our street too," she recalled. "People changed through the arithmetic of birth, marriage and death, but not by going away. So families just accrued stories, which through the fullness of time, in those times, their own lives made. And I grew up on those."

After college in Mississippi and in the North, she worked as a photographer for the Work Projects Administration during the Depression, taking pictures for a guide to Mississippi. She also wrote for a radio station and a newspaper until her fiction began to become popular and she could earn her living as a writer.

Her literary mentor was fellow southern belle, Katherine Anne Porter. In addition to her novels and short stories, Eudora is well known for the autobiographical *One Writer's Beginnings* and a fabulous book on writing called *The Eye of the Story.*

She gave up photography as a career, she recalled once in an essay entitled "One Time, One Place," because she realized that "a fuller awareness of what I needed to find out about people and their lives had to be sought for through another way, through writing stories. . . . [and] my wish, indeed my continuing passion, would be not to point the finger in judgment but to part a curtain, that invisible shadow that falls between people, the veil of indifference to each other's presence, each other's wonder, each other's human plight." Our literary heritage is richer for her decision.

SISTER

Among the southern characters **Eudora Welty** is famous for immortalizing is Sister in "Why I Live at the P.O." Sister is a maiden aunt, that southern fixture who was seen as an indispensable member of the family circle but denied the social status accorded to mothers and grandmothers. Doling out advice, comfort, punishment, and a listening ear, the maiden aunt was often dependent on her married relatives for financial support. Aunt Pittypat in *Gone With the Wind* is another such figure.

A FORCE TO BE RECKONED WITH

"*You*'re going to be famous," Billie Holiday told **Maya Angelou** in 1958, "but it won't be for singing." Billie was prophetic. Mute as a child, Maya Angelou has gone on to become one of the most powerful voices in American society today. Who can ever forget that powerful, precise voice that dominated the 1993 inauguration of president Bill Clinton as she recited "On the Pulse of Morning?"

Her journey from silence to worldwide acclaim is an amazing one, told by her in five autobiographical volumes: *I Know Why the Caged Bird Sings, Gather Together in My Name, Singin' and Swingin' and Gettin' Merry Like Christmas, The Heart of a Woman,* and *All God's Children Need Traveling Shoes.* She was born Marguerite Johnson in St. Louis in 1928, but at age three was sent to live with her paternal grandmother in Stamps, Arkansas, a town so segregated that many black children, she claimed, "didn't, really, absolutely know what whites looked like."

"'Thou shall not be dirty' and 'Thou shall not be impudent' were the two commandments of Grandmother Henderson upon which hung our total salvation," she remembers in *I Know Why the Caged Bird Sings.* "Each night in the bitterest winter we were forced to wash faces, arms, necks, legs and feet before going to bed. She used to add, with a smirk that unprofane people can't control when venturing into profanity, 'and wash as far as possible, then wash possible.'"

When she was seven, on a visit to her mother, she was raped by her mother's boyfriend, which she reported to her mother. The man was tried and sent to jail, which confused and upset the young girl. When he was killed in prison for being a child molester, she felt responsible and spent the next five years in total silence.

With the help of her grandmother and another woman, Bertha Flowers, who introduced her to literature, Maya slowly came out of herself, graduating at the top of her eighth grade class, and moved to San Francisco to live in her mother's boarding house. She went to school, took dance and drama lessons, and in her spare time, became the first African American streetcar conductor in San Francisco. An unplanned pregnancy at sixteen made her a mother and she later had a short-lived marriage with Tosh Angelos, still later adapting his surname and taking as her first name the nickname her brother used for her. Working at a variety of odd jobs (including a madam for two lesbian prostitutes), she eventually began to make a living as a singer and dancer. In 1954, she toured Europe and Africa for the State Department in *Porgy and Bess*. Upon returning to the United States, she created a revue *Cabaret for Freedom*, as a benefit for Martin

Luther King, Jr.'s Southern Christian Leadership Conference (SCLC). Later she served as the northern coordinator for the SCLC at Dr. King's request.

In 1961, she left the United States with her son and her lover, Vusumzi Make, a South African freedom fighter, to live in Cairo, where she tried to become the editor of the *Arab Observer*. The Egyptians wouldn't think of a woman in the position and her lover was equally outraged. She left him and moved to Ghana, where she lived for five years, working as an editor and writer for various newspapers and teaching at the University of Ghana. She loved the people of Ghana: "their skins were the colors of my childhood cravings: peanut butter, licorice, chocolate, caramel. There was the laughter of home, quick and without artifice," she wrote in *All God's Children Need Traveling Shoes*. But she never felt completely accepted and returned to the U.S. in 1966.

She began writing books at the urging of James Baldwin, who had heard her tell her childhood stories and encouraged her to write them down. (Another story has it that it was a chance meeting with cartoonist Jules Feiffer that was the impetus.) But the multi-talented dynamo continued to act in both plays and films and began to write poetry and plays as well. In 1972, she became the first African American woman to have a screenplay produced—*Georgia, Georgia*—and she won an Emmy nomination for her performance in *Roots*. When *I Know Why the Caged Bird Sings* was made into a TV movie, Maya wrote the script—and the music. She also wrote and produced a ten-part TV series on African traditions in American life. She has received many honorary degrees, serves on the board of trustees of the American Film Institute, and is Reynolds Professor of American Studies at Wake Forest University in Winston-Salem, North Carolina.

Her autobiographies have been criticized for not being completely factual, to which she once replied, "There's a world of difference between truth and facts. Facts can obscure the truth. You can tell so many facts that you fill the stage but haven't gotten one iota of truth." She is deeply respected for her amazing capacity not merely to survive, but to triumph. Maya Angelou, one of the most celebrated authors of the 20th century, is certainly a moral force to be reckoned with.

Other Stellar Literary Belles

- **Frances Hodgson Burnett,** beloved author of *The Secret Garden* and *A Little Princess,* had to pick grapes near her Knoxville, Tennessee, home to make enough money to buy the pen and paper for her first story

- **Marguerite Henry,** immortalized children's literature and the wild horses on a Virginia island, in *Misty of Chincoteague*

- Outspoken liberal **Lillian Smith** rocked the South (and was banned in Boston) with her 1944 bestseller set in Georgia, *Strange Fruit,* that depicted a love affair between an educated black woman and the son of a white doctor (the story was inspired by Billie Holiday's tragic blues)

- **Kate Chopin** was known best at the turn of the 20th century for portraying Creole life in Louisiana in *The Awakening,* which scandalized readers in 1899 with a tale of extramarital interracial love that has now been hailed as an early feminist novel of a woman's search for herself

- Kentucky novelist **Harriette Arnow's** (born 1908) most famous work, *The Dollmaker,* was later made into a movie starring Jane Fonda

- **Fanny Kemble** (1809-1893) married plantation owner Pierce Butler, but divorced him after fourteen years because she was horrified at slavery and went on to pen two famous antislavery tracts

- **Pearl S. Buck,** born in Hillsboro, West Virginia, but raised in China by her missionary parents, was the only woman to have ever won the Pulitzer Prize *and* the Nobel Prize for Literature for *The Good Earth*

DEAR DOROTHY...

If you cringe every time you read the advice doled out by Ann Landers or her sister Abby Dearest, take heart in knowing that the root of all advice columns was none other than the dyed-in-the-wool southern feminist (before they knew what that meant) **Dorothy Dix.** Dorothy, born in 1861 with the name Elizabeth Gilmer, came from an old Tennessee family and taught herself about the world by devouring virtually the entire impressive library that her father had built up. As an adult, she fell into a disastrous marriage which eventually ended with her husband dying in a mental institution. Fortunately, her father was able to support her.

Then, in the serendipitous way that life often metes out its rewards, Elizabeth had a nervous breakdown in 1890; and her father rushed her off to the Mississippi gulf coast town of Bay Saint Louis to recover. While there, she happened to meet Eliza Nicholson, the wife of the owner of the *New Orleans Daily Picayune,* and when she was introduced to Eliza's husband, she told him of her interest in newspaper work. He encouraged her, and, by 1894, she was living in New Orleans and working on the paper. Her first column, under her pen name of Dorothy Dix, appeared in 1895. A sharp, caustic, yet witty style characterized her pieces, many of which were concerned with women's issues (like one of her earliest columns titled "Give the Girls a Chance").

She didn't set out to write an advice column, but she was an instant hit, particularly with women readers who began writing letters to her at the *Picayune* asking for advice. Dorothy obliged and so was born the genre. Her fame became astronomical when later, in the heyday of splashy murder coverage, Dorothy took some time off from armchair therapy to become one of William Randolph Hearst's more celebrated crime reporters. Her ability to empathize with the accused, as well as the victim, enabled her to get more revealing interviews and captured the imagination of the entire salivating nation.

But sensational murder trials got old and her heart was still in the South, particularly in responding to the increasingly large number of letters she got begging for advice. She returned to New Orleans and writing for the *Picayune* until her death in 1951. To Dorothy, answering the pleas of her audience wasn't just a question of finding good copy. It was an act of sacred obligation; indeed, she was overwhelmed with sacks of mail and still insisted on personally answering each letter. She empathized greatly with her female audience, which came across in the pieces she wrote. The empathy was sincere, for she heartily believed, as she once said, that being a woman was "the most arduous profession any human being could follow."

BAD ADVICE NOT TAKEN

It seems that to get by as a southern woman writer it was often a prerequisite to ignore all the advice you got from men. In her autobiography, *The Woman Within,* **Ellen Glasgow** tells of the "help" she once received: "In the end, as in the beginning, Mr. Collier (a noted figure on the American literary scene) gave me no encouragement. 'The best advice I can give you,' he said, with charming candor, 'is to stop writing, and go back to the South and have some babies . . . The greatest woman is not the woman who has written the finest book, but the woman who has had the finest babies.'" Fortunately, Ellen Glasgow, born in 1873 in Richmond, Virginia, and deaf by the time she was twenty, ignored Collier's advice. Instead she became a prolific writer, winning the Pulitzer Prize in 1942 for her novel, *In This Our Life.*

Her Heart Was A Lonely Hunter

*B*eing anointed as the next great southern talent is a hell of a burden, particularly if you are only twenty-three years old, eccentric, and slightly emotionally unbalanced to boot. But **Lula Carson Smith McCullers** was a serious talent. Writing became her fixation early on after her diligently pursued, but still-fantasy, career as a pianist faded after suffering from a severe bout with rheumatic fever. Her first major work was a play full of murder, incest, and bizarre behavior that she attempted to produce in her family drawing room; but, according to the future literary genius, "only my mother and my eleven-year-old sister would cooperate."

At seventeen, having dropped the "Lula" for the more literary "Carson," she, like so many of her contemporaries, fled the South for the big cities of the North, ostensibly to study music at Julliard and writing at Columbia. Things went awry, however, and she spent the next two years working in New York before retreating to Georgia, after being felled for a second time by rheumatic fever. While recovering, "Choppers" (as she was secretly referred to by Tennessee Williams because her face looked like two pork chops) worked on what would become her first book and courted Reeves McCullers. They were married in 1937 and moved to Fayetteville, North Carolina, where Reeves had a job waiting.

By 1940, their marriage already showing signs of serious strain, they moved to New York. Carson's first novel, *The Heart Is a Lonely Hunter*, came out to enthusiastic praise later that year, winning the Pulitzer, and earning her the "next great" label she would struggle against for the rest of her life. Within the next ten years, she would get divorced, remarry, separate again, alienate much of the literary community with her mercurial emotional outbursts, grovel for love and then impulsively toss it away, reunite with her ex only to break up again and, through it all, write, write, write. Between 1940 and 1951, she produced the works that would stand the test of time: the novels, *The Heart Is a Lonely Hunter* (1940), *Reflections In a Golden Eye* (1941), *The Member of the Wedding* (1950), and *The Ballad of the Sad Cafe* (1951), and a smattering of short stories of which one, "A Tree, A Rock, A Cloud," was awarded the O. Henry Award in 1942.

While widely critically acclaimed and even characterized by writer Gore Vidal as "*the* young writer" of her time, Carson's health and emotional life, never terribly stable to begin with, were slowly coming apart. Her on-again-off-again marriage ended in 1953 when Reeves killed himself in Paris. The next decade produced no writing worthy of her abilities; and she died in 1967 at the age of fifty after ten years of serious health problems and a number of literary failures.

GREAT FEMALE CHARACTERS FROM THE SOUTH

Bone Boatwright
Bastard Out of Carolina by Dorothy Allison

Holly Golightly
Breakfast at Tiffany's by Truman Capote

Scarlett O'Hara
Gone With the Wind by Margaret Mitchell

Blanche Dubois
A Streetcar Named Desire by Tennessee Williams

Emily
A Rose for Emily by William Faulkner

Sister
"Why I Live at the P.O." by Eudora Welty

Miss Minerva
Miss Minerva and William Green Hill
by Frances Boyd Calhoun

Celie
The Color Purple by Alice Walker

THE HARD-BOILED VIRGIN

For many an educated lady in the 19th century South, the only open career avenues were teaching and tending the books at the library. For **Frances Newman,** born and raised in post-civil war Atlanta, her journey to the dusty shelves of the Carnegie Library proved the opening she needed to scandalize much of her hometown and build a breathtaking foundation to a literary career that was cut tragically short.

While working at the library, Frances began writing reviews for library journals and the local Atlanta newspapers. Her powerful prose and sharp wit caught the attention of then-reigning literary master H. L. Mencken, who encouraged her to continue to write. Her very first short story was published in *Mencken's* magazine and brought Frances immediate recognition, winning the O. Henry Award for best short story.

Frances' first novel, *The Hard-Boiled Virgin*, was a bawdy tale of a woman of many affairs. It caused great consternation in Atlanta, where everyone was convinced—wrongly—that it was autobiographical. The scandal, however, did boost book sales considerably, for which Frances was grateful. She also succeeded in accomplishing a badge of honor for many Southern women writers—her book was banned in Boston.

Her second novel, the equally provocative sounding *Dead Lovers are Faithful Lovers*, was published in 1928. What her next literary moves might have been will never be known, for Frances died suddenly later that year at age forty-five of a ruptured cerebral aneurysm.

AN UNREALIZED TALENT

*Z*elda Sayre Fitzgerald, the South's favorite manic depressive, went straight from the quiet streets of Montgomery, Alabama, to the front page of the *New York Times* style section. Alongside her equally glittering husband, F. Scott Fitzgerald, she was like a shooting star heralding the initiation of a new age between the two world wars by living the fantasy-life dreamt of by millions. And like a shooting star, she shone brightly with spectacular, even breathtaking, appeal and then burned out—literally. Zelda died at the age of forty-eight in a fire at a mental institution, after a twenty- year-long battle with her inner demons.

Named by her mother after a Gypsy queen in a novel she had read, Zelda seemed destined for glamour from the beginning. Stories of her antics circulated through Montgomery for decades after she had flown the coop for the big time. Like the time young Zelda got bored on a Saturday afternoon and called the fire department to alert them to a poor young girl trapped on a roof top and then proceeded to climb up onto her roof, kick the ladder down, and wait in glee for rescue. From the time she was born, she seemed always in a rush to get somewhere she could never quite reach.

Raised on "The Hill," the heart of Alabama's stubborn attempt to cling to the ways of the antebellum south, Zelda had all the credentials of a proper southern lady—buttoned-up white gloves and all. But she and her siblings (of whom Scott once commented that the only real resemblance between them was that they were all unstable), grew up largely unattended. From early on, Zelda was the life of every party and the creator of most—in her senior year at high school she organized an April Fool's Day prank where the entire senior class took the day off.

Always referred to as a rare golden-haired beauty, much of her magnetic attraction came from the unpredictable strength of her intensity—the sense that she could, and would, do anything at any moment. She won the hearts of half the boys in Alabama and most of the Yankee officer corps stationed around Montgomery in 1917. (There was an attempt by some of the older gentlemen of the area to socially freeze out the Yankees, but it didn't fly with the young women in town.) Within three years, Zelda married Scott, whose first novel, *This Side of Paradise*, appeared to much acclaim; and they were

off on a wild ride of transatlantic partying that would capture the imagination of the entire country. From the Riviera to New York, back to Paris, and on to Washington, they always stayed at the best hotels, surrounded by society's most glamorous people, living out images from Scott's very own novels.

Zelda became the glamorous "First Flapper" of the Jazz Age, an era her husband had named and described as "a new generation grown up to find all gods dead, all wars fought, all faiths in man shaken." Hidden behind the glittering front page parade, however, was a woman talented in her own right, as a writer (brilliant but undisciplined, according to her husband) and a painter. More tragic were the buried seeds of mental illness that began to emerge as early as 1925, when she collapsed while in Paris, leading her to begin a series of prolonged "treatments." In between the parties and the emotional breakdowns, she managed to write a novel called *Save Me the Waltz*, which critics believe demonstrated her great promise.

By 1930, the shooting star that was Zelda's life had sputtered into darkness. Her seclusion in a series of mental institutions was broken up by brief periods where she would return to her family, filled with her legendary passion for life. Some critics have suggested that the strain of living in "The Jazz Age," while carrying the burden of the manufactured southern belle deep within her, contributed to her problems. Zelda herself once wrote "it is very difficult to be two simple people at once, one who wants to have a law to itself and the other who wants to keep all the nice old things and be loved and safe and protected." Sadly, it is believed that, had she lived in the present day of modern medical miracles, her terrible bouts and sensitive emotional condition could have been treated with simple medication.

FRIGID AS A CUCUMBER?

*K*atherine Ann Porter was a fabulous storyteller, penning some of the best short stories and novels around: *Ship of Fools; Pale Horse, Pale Rider;* and *Flowering Judas and Other Stories.* She also used her remarkable talent to remake the story of her life, noted Enrique Lopez in *Conversations with Katherine Ann Porter,* confusing "the romantic desires of the past and the fancies of the moment with realities that were too much to recognize in the harsh light of day. Perhaps that was the prerogative of the southern lady. . . . To embroider a bit, to change the facts to fit the storyteller's mood or the hearer's fancy."

Born in 1890 in Indian Creek, Texas, she lost her mother at a very young age and was raised by a stern father, a great-great-grandnephew of Daniel Boone, who instilled in her a love of books. Her family was originally from Kentucky and Louisiana and, throughout her life, she felt keenly the effects of her family's post-Civil War reversal of fortune: "I am a grandchild of a lost War, and I have blood-knowledge of what life can be in a defeated country on the bare bones of privation."

Educated at a Catholic convent in New Orleans, she demonstrated her rebellious spirit early. On Saturdays, when the girls were allowed to go to town, she and her sister would attend the horse races. "I have always had a penchant for long odds and black horses with poetic names," she later commented, "no matter what their past records indicated." At sixteen she wed, but was so fearful of sex, she refused to consummate the marriage. She divorced three years later and was forty-two before she married again. "I was frigid as a cucumber," she recalled, "and never really did get over it altogether." Despite such assertions, however, she is rumored to have had many lovers and had three husbands in all.

Eventually she moved to Chicago and then Greenwich Village, leaving Texas far behind because "I didn't want to be regarded as a freak. That's what they all thought about women who wanted to write. So I had to revolt and rebel; there was no other way." Extremely beautiful, with unblemished ivory skin and bow lips, the sharp-tongued writer had more than her share of male admirers. "As so frequently happens with beautiful southern women," notes Lopez, "many would-be suitors were so charmed by her voice they paid only minimal heed to what she was saying, consequently ignoring . . . the bite in her humor, which inevitably convinced her that 'it's often difficult to insult a fool.'"

Over her long life (she died at age ninety), she was often where the action was. Lovers with Diego Rivera, she befriended and smoked pot with Mexican revolutionaries in the 1920s, and was jailed in Boston for protesting the Sacco and Vanzetti trial. She dined with Göring and Goebbels in the 1930s (where, she claimed later, she told them that the Nazi's "hatred of Jews is a kind of national sickness"). Later she befriended such authors as Hart Crane, Robert Penn Warren, and Truman Capote, whose "party of the century" she refused to attend upon learning that she was to be seated with other elderly folks. Her retort: "Nothing could have been more deadly than getting together with a bunch of people as old as I am." Once, when Christopher Isherwood called her "a Texas Joan of Arc," the then fifty-five-year-old Katherine Ann pulled his hair — hard. This prompted Norman Mailer to declare her, "about the meanest little old lady in tennis shoes I've ever met. And I guess you know that hair-pulling is a sure sign of sexual frustration."

After a lifetime of struggle to make ends meet, at age seventy-two, she hit the jackpot with *Ship of Fools*, which, while it failed to reap the awards many thought the long-awaited novel deserved (she worked on it off-and-on for eighteen years), did earn her worldwide celebrity and a million dollars in royalties and film rights. She wrote almost up to her death, although she failed in her desire, in true Texas style, "to die with my boots on — I want to be working full tilt at my typewriter, so that I'll be in the middle of a sentence when the end comes."

66A house is just like a man — you ought to live with it at least a year before deciding on anything permanent. And even then it's a big gamble.**99**
    —*Katherine Ann Porter*

BREAKING THE SILENCE

When Atlantan **Rosemary Daniell's** first collection of poems, *A Sexual Tour of the Deep South,* (Holt, Rhinehart and Winston, 1975), and later when her first memoir, *Fatal Flowers: On Sin, Sex and Suicide in the Deep South.* (Henry Holt, & Company, 1989: Holt, Rhinehart and Winston, 1980) were published, they shocked both her hometown and the country with her honest portrayals of the two experiences that had formerly been forbidden expression to southern women in literature: anger and sexuality. Rosemary says that her decision to explore these forbidden areas was inspired by her mother, Melissa, a beautiful Southern woman — one of those brought up to believe that "if you can't say something nice, don't say anything at all" — who was also a talented writer who thought she didn't have the right to be, and who ended her life by suicide.

THE QUEEN OF THE DAMNED

*W*hat would make a good Irish Catholic girl, write about vampires, model her main bloodsucker, Lestat, after the male version of herself, and, in her spare time write some of the steamiest sadomasochistic adult erotica on the market? It might have started as a reaction to being pegged with the name Howard Allen Frances O'Brien by her loving parents; but then again, it's not all that unusual for someone growing up in New Orleans. Before she was ever humiliated on the playground, **Anne Rice** dumped the Howard Allen and, after a few years of rapid name change experimentation, finally settled on just plain Anne. But since then she's done a fine job of proving there is nothing plain or ordinary about Anne Rice.

Born in 1941, Anne had the good fortune of being brought up in one of the most uniquely interesting cities in the world, haunted by its charm and mystery. In 1956, when she was just a teenager, her mother died of alcohol abuse. After a brief stay in Texas, where her father relocated, she met poet Stan Rice, whom she married in 1961. From 1964 through 1988, she lived in the San Francisco Bay Area, alternately writing, working odd jobs, soaking up the west coast's version of quirk and old world charm, and going to school.

In 1972, her daughter Michele (affectionately called "Mouse") died of leukemia. During the seven years that followed, Anne worked on *Interview With the Vampire* — a novel featuring child vampire Claudia, a character based on her deceased daughter. After repeated rejection, the novel was finally published in the mid-1970s to wild acclaim. The mix of horror, blood, sexual tension, and romantic settings proved a potent, wealth-producing combination; and the prolific Anne has continued to crank out several bestselling series of books dealing with vampires, witches, demons, mummies, and ghosts. Her books have given her the opportunity to revisit her beloved characters and her hometown, again and again. In addition, under the pen names Ann Rampling and A.N. Roquelaure, she has also dabbled in erotica, penning such works as *Exit to Eden* and *Sleeping Beauty*.

Her penchant for having a good time has included a season of book-signings where she wore wedding dresses to all of her appearances, including a special affair in New Orleans where she arrived via coffin in an old world Quarter-style jazz funeral procession. But, more often than not, these shenanigans have resulted in the media's glossing over of the deeper, more penetrating, and powerful themes found in her work. This distresses her, as she once pointed out in her fan club newsletter, because she uses her "other-worldly characters to delve more deeply into the heart of guilt, love, alienation, bisexuality, loss of grace [and] terror in a meaningless universe."

Her fame is extraordinary; and she created quite a stir a few years ago when she criticized the casting of Tom Cruise as Lestat in the movie version of *Interview with the Vampire* (she later recanted). Recently she bought the former St. Elizabeth's Orphanage, a massive old structure that takes up an entire square block in New Orleans and is in the process of bringing it back to life in a new incarnation as one part home, one part museum, and one part fun house. In 1995, she hosted the annual coven party started by her legion of fans from the Vampire Lestat Fan Club at her "orphanage." With a little luck, inspired by our fascination with the unknown, and propelled by a multitude of fans worldwide, Anne Rice will continue to turn out her luminous, demon-filled view of the world for years to come.

Peggy O'Hara? Pansy O'Hara?
Scarlett O'Hara

The fiery red-headed, Irish southern belle whose family typified the antebellum South had been through a terrible war, seen her home town of Atlanta burnt in an uncontrollable conflagration, and lived to see the day when the streets of Atlanta were filled with soldiers. No, it wasn't Scarlett O'Hara, but her creator and alter ego whose family were central characters in the history of Georgia.

Born in 1900, **Margaret Mitchell** came of age during the great mobilization of World War I. Her mother was feminist Maybelle Mitchell, a noted suffragist and founder of the Atlanta Women's Study Club; "nothing infuriated her so much," reported Margaret later, "as the complacent attitude of other ladies who felt they should let the gentlemen do the voting." She immortalized Mama in her famous novel, modeling the character of Rhett Butler after the tough-minded Maybelle.

A former flapper (using her maiden name in a belle-ish manner very uncharacteristic of genteel southern ladies in the early decades of the century), Margaret began writing her epic novel in 1926, after a serious ankle injury ended her brief career as Peggy Mitchell, columnist for the *Atlanta Journal*. Never intended for publication, *Gone With the Wind* was instead viewed by Margaret as a very private exercise, where she could weave together many of the stories that surrounded her. The manuscript evolved over a period of ten years into a massive cluttered stack of disjointed papers. She rarely spoke about it to anyone, although after awhile the existence of this huge pile of words became common knowledge among her friends: one of whom included MacMillian editor Harold Latham, who, in a 1935 visit to Atlanta, asked Margaret if he could take a look at it.

Impulsively, and in retrospect, surprisingly, for someone who considered herself a poor writer and was extremely private about her writing, Margaret bundled up the huge stack of handwritten pages and dumped them onto his lap. Almost immediately she had second thoughts and, when Harold got back to New York, he found a telegram informing him that she had changed her mind and to send the manuscript back. By then, he had already become ensnared in the saga (even though at the time it lacked a first chapter and any semblance of order).

The rest, as they say, is history. *Gone With the Wind* was published in 1936 and its huge (over one thousand pages) romantic saga of struggle and perseverance immediately captured the imagination of the Depression-battered public, becoming a monumental bestseller. It was also the last book Margaret Mitchell would write (she had previously written parts of two novellas, one called *Pansy Hamilton Flapper Heroine* and the other *Ropa Carmagin*, but both remained unpublished and were destroyed after her death by her family). In 1996, *Lost Laysen*, another previously lost novella, was published by her estate; but it failed to capture the same attention of her greatest work.

The sheer scope of impact that *Gone With the Wind* has made on the American cultural landscape is breathtaking. In many respects, due to its incredibly evocative description of the antebellum South, it has come to represent the exact opposite of what Margaret intended. Instead of a simple story about a young girl learning how to grow into a strong woman with her own identity, who is able to rely on her own wits and succeed, it became for many the one-sided symbol of nostalgia for a particular period in history that existed for a small elite group of slave owners, not at all typical of most Southerners of the time.

When asked her opinion about what made *Gone With the Wind* such a success, Margaret opined: "Despite its length and many details, *Gone With the Wind* is basically just a simple yarn of fairly simple people. There's no fine writing; there are no grandiose thoughts; there are no hidden meanings, no symbolism, nothing sensational—nothing, nothing at all that have made other bestsellers bestsellers. Then how to explain its appeal from the five year old to the ninety-five year old? I can't figure it out."

Margaret Mitchell, in true fashion of the free-spirited, strong-willed, independent, archetypal female character she created, went on to endow a medical chair providing full scholarships for African American students that has helped to create some of the best doctors in the United States. By the time she was tragically killed by a speeding taxi cab on Peachtree Street in Atlanta at the age of forty-eight, Margaret's greatness, on the basis of one book, was cemented forever in history.

THE ULTIMATE HOLLYWOOD LEGEND

You know you're big when they model a Barbie after you. There have been plenty of Scarlett dolls through the years, but the 1994 Barbie version was the biggest hit. Reputed to be the most authentically costumed, "Gone With the Wind" Barbie came in four versions of Scarlett: the white and green barbecue dress, the green velvet drapery dress, the red velveteen gown with beads and feathers, and the black and white honeymoon outfit. (There was also a Ken as Rhett in a black tuxedo and cape.)

Calling all Scarletts

Do you have an eighteen-inch waist or an affinity for clothing made from draperies? Big jug ears or an American Express card reading Captain Rhett Butler? You too can be a Rhett or Scarlett impersonator! Throughout the South, dozens of women and men work full (and part) time as impersonators of the infamous duo from *Gone With the Wind*. Impersonating the famous movie characters is a lucrative business—a good Rhett or Scarlett can command between $125 and $150 dollars an hour (with a two hour minimum), hired out for corporate parties, receptions, and even trips abroad. In fact, professional faux-Scarlett and multi-linguist Melly Meadows, a dead-ringer for Vivien Leigh, once shocked a visiting Japanese businessman and the surrounding on lookers by answering his query about her in his native tongue. Bet that's one thing they never heard of at Tara!

❝ The usual masculine disillusionment is in discovering that a woman has a brain. ❞
—*Margaret Mitchell,* Gone With the Wind

Her Eyes Were Watching God

*Z*ora **Neale Hurston** no doubt earned the frustration of many of her contemporaries since, for her, the struggles over civil rights that dominated her lifetime, were side issues. In *How It Feels to Be Me*, one of her earliest essays, she wrote: "I do not belong to the sobbing school of Negrohood who hold down that nature somehow has given them a low-down dirty deal and whose feelings are all hurt about it. Even in the helter-skelter skirmish that is my life, I have seen that the world is to the strong regardless of a little pigmentation more or less. I do not weep at the world—I am too busy sharpening my oyster knife."

Born in 1891 (or 1901—Zora Neale played loose with the dates), she went on to become a central chronicler of African American culture. Raised by a firebrand of a mother in Eatonville, Florida, she traveled to Howard University in Atlanta and then on to Harlem in the early 1920s to become a part of the growing Harlem Renaissance. A visible part of this northern cultural movement, her heart was never really far above the Mason-Dixon line. In New York, Zora Neale's writings won her a scholarship to Barnard College and later a graduate degree from Columbia, where she studied under the famous anthropologist Franz Boas. Franz encouraged her to study the folklore of the diaspora of African Americans and that suggestion became her life's passion.

Her first collection of folk stories, *Mules and Men*, came from tales she collected in Alabama and Florida between 1929 and 1931. Its publication was greeted with great enthusiasm by the academic press; but, in a theme that would repeat itself throughout her life, she was criticized bitterly by some black reviewers for painting "too rosy" a picture of African American life and failing to include the degradation and shame of daily existence. Zora Neale's championing of black culture would get her into deeper trouble towards the end of her life, when she blasted the Supreme Court's school desegregation decision as an affront to the value of black institutions.

Her most noted novel, *Their Eyes Were Watching God* (1937), is a poignant tale of a black woman's sexual and spiritual yearnings. Her autobiography, *Dust Tracks On a Road*, was published in 1942; and she also produced a series of short ethnographic films of rural black existence. The films currently reside in a University of California library and are occasionally exhibited.

Opinionated and single-minded, Zora Neale was married twice, but both marriages ended in divorce when she refused to give up her traveling and collecting folk stories, to be a stay-at-home wife. She fell into poverty in the 1950s as book sales fell off, and died alone and penniless in Fort Pierce, Florida, in 1960. She was buried in a grave in a seg-regated cemetery which remained unmarked until writer Alice Walker erected a stone marker at its site in 1973 reading: "Zora Neale Hurston, 1901-1960. A Genius of the South, Novelist, Folklorist, Anthropologist." Ironically, in the last twenty-five years, sales of Zora Neale's works have soared through the well-publicized interest of others like Alice Walker and Oprah Winfrey, bringing her great acclaim and her estate great riches, both of which she was denied during her lifetime.

❝ The best thing to do is grab the broom of anger and drive off the fear. **❞**
   —Zora Neale Hurston

2

Confederate Cut-Ups
and
One Revolutionary Rebel

They stood by the South—or at least most of them did anyway—and took action, proving that southern women have grit and guts when the going gets rough.

THE SCOURGE OF THE BRITISH

Stories of **Nancy Hart** abound and, as the authors of *Georgia Women* note, it is often hard to separate fact from fiction. One of the main problems appears to be that there were, in fact, two Nancy Harts.

The first Nancy Hart was a red-headed, hard swearing, six-foot tall, fearsome sharpshooter (reputed to have been cross-eyed) born in 1735, who was the scourge of the British during the Revolutionary War. Little is know about her early life, except that her family was related to Daniel Boone; and at some point, she married Benjamin Hart. The two moved to 400 acres in the Broad River area of Georgia in Wilkes (now Elbert) County, which became known as the Hornets' Nest due to Nancy and her freedom fightin' friends.

But before the troubles began, Benjamin farmed "under the whip of Nancy's sharp tongue," claims *Great Georgians,* going on to note that Nancy obviously "wore the pants in the family. One neighbor is quoted as saying, 'Poor Nancy, she was a honey of a Patriot, but the devil of a wife.'" Her acumen with a gun, however, produced many a meal for the couple and their eight children; and earned her the nickname "War Woman" from neighboring Native Americans.

When the Revolutionary War broke out and the British, having captured Savannah and Augusta, were heading her way, Big Nan refused to evacuate her home and offered her services as a spy and a soldier to General Elijah Clarke. Not one to take no for an answer, Nancy dressed as a man and infiltrated British forces, where, under the ruse of insanity, she obtained vital information that helped lead to a major American victory.

The most famous story about Nancy Hart recounts how she captured six Tories singlehandedly, after lulling them into a false sense of security with food and drink. While

they were imbibing, she started handing their rifles out through a chink in her cabin wall to her daughter waiting outside. When the men discovered what was happening, she grabbed a gun and held them at bay while her daughter ran for help. Though many versions exist of what happened next, eventually her husband and rescue arrived; and the Tories were taken outside and hung, to the tune of "Yankee Doodle Dandy."

After her husband's death, she remarried and moved West. But Georgians still claim her proudly and have honored her by naming a city, a county, a creek, a locomotive, a school, and a highway after her. The Nancy Hart Highway is one of the few interstates named for a woman in the U.S. You can find a marker in her honor on Georgia Highway 17, about ten miles south of Elberton; but she remains in the hearts and lore of Georgia forever.

AND WHAT OF THE OTHER NANCY?

She hailed from West Virginia and served as a guide for a Confederate captain in the Civil War. Legend has it that she was also six foot tall (highly unlikely, probably some confusion with Nancy I), but beautiful. Caught once by Yankees, she convinced them that she was just an innocent southern belle and was let go. But that didn't end her spying career and eventually Union leaders put a $500 price (a staggering sum at the time) on her head. Captured again in Summersville, West Virginia, she was imprisoned in an attic with a guard, who kept threatening to throw her out of the window. She managed to escape and exacted her revenge by having Confederate troops burn the town while she kidnapped her former guard, outfitted him in one of her dresses, and paraded him through town tethered to the back of her horse.

SKIRTING DISASTER

Emeline Pigott is credited with finding a useful purpose for the hoop skirts that were the required apparel of southern women in the middle of the 19th century—they hid her courier's pouch as she worked her way between Union and Confederate lines passing information to the Confederacy.

Born into a North Carolina family with deep roots in Carteret County, Emeline's teenage years were spent conversing with the Confederate soldiers camped around her family farm. Courted by many of the officers, she instead fell madly and tragically in love with a private named Stokes MacRae. When MacRae was killed in the Battle of Gettysburg, Emeline vowed to spend the rest of her life working for the Confederate cause.

At first retreating with the fleeing army and helping as a field nurse, she soon dressed up in her finest and worked her way back home across enemy lines. Back in Carteret County, Emeline helped sneak provisions to Confederate soldiers hiding in the forest and soon graduated to courier work, acting as a conduit to connect the splintered Confederate forces in the region with messages, medicine, and letters.

Apparently Emeline's all too familiar hoop-skirted figure finally caught the eye of Union troops, who set out to entrap her by having a couple of questionable characters in Beaufort plant "military secrets" upon her person. She was arrested before she ever got out of town, but managed to delay the immodest invasion of her hoops by insisting that the task be performed by a woman to whom she had been properly introduced. While the Union officers scrambled to dig up an acquaintance, Emeline managed to swallow the most incriminating evidence and shred the remaining letters. She was arrested anyway.

She spent a month in prison, survived an assassination attempt and the torment of being hauled into court on a daily basis, to face the almost certain sentence of death for spying. Then, inexplicably, she was allowed to return home. Some say she threatened the two men who had set her up with certain death if she were not set free, while others believe the Union Army thought they could get more out of her by letting her loose and watching her every move. For whatever reason, she was freed, and though greatly restricted in her movement, immediately returned to doing everything possible to help her beloved Confederacy.

Emeline Pigott stayed faithful to her love and her cause to the bitter end. She never married and was buried next to an unknown Confederate soldier, whose grave she had tended all her post-war life.

Laughter Isn't Always the Best Medicine

New Orleans resident **Eugenia Phillips** was loyal to the Confederacy and engaged in espionage — or at least Union officials thought the mother of eight to be. So in 1862, when she laughed at a Union military funeral cortege passing by her home, she was imprisoned. During her confinement, she stoically lived for several months in a ramshackle cabin near a mosquito bog, protesting her innocence, until she was finally released for lack of evidence.

THE FIRST LADY OF DIXIE

*S*he was the First (and only) Lady of the Confederacy. But, according to Joan Cashin in an article in *Portraits of American Women*, **Varina Jefferson Davis,** born in 1826 and raised outside Natchez, Mississippi, was often accused of being neither "'Ladylike' in her dress or conduct nor a 'truehearted southern woman.'" She was also considered "imperious." Perhaps her bad reputation had to do with her being educated in Philadelphia. Or maybe it was her harsh, often sarcastic, sense of humor, thought to be so unbecoming in a proper southern lady. Or perhaps the fact that she fought openly with her husband's brother over the title to land that she believed to rightly belong to Jefferson brought on her detractors—Jefferson's brother, Joseph, even wrote a will specifically preventing Varina from ever inheriting the disputed land. Or maybe her husband's political enemies were just spreading ill will. Whatever the cause, Varina never spoke badly of the South and defended her husband to the end.

She was nineteen when she wed the thirty-six-year-old Jefferson Davis. Three years later, she moved to Washington D.C., where her husband was a newly elected member of the House of Representatives, and for the next twelve years, greatly enjoyed the social life that Washingtonians revel in. She also gave birth to four children, but ran into trouble from southern women for continuing to have "fun" while she was pregnant, a delicate state indeed. When Jefferson was named president of the Confederacy, they moved first to Montgomery, Alabama, and then to Richmond, Virginia.

A good friend of Mary Boykin Chestnut, Varina was no dummy. She confided to her mother in Mississippi in a letter that "the North has a great advantage in manufacturing power" and that her husband was "depressed" about the prospects for the Confederacy. Nonetheless, when she was asked to flee Richmond in 1865, she wrote, "Very adverse to flight and unwilling at all times to leave him, I argued the question with him and pleaded to be permitted to remain, until he said, 'I have confidence in your capacity to take care of our babies, and understand your desire to assist and comfort me, but you can do this in but one way, and that is by going yourself and taking our children to a place of safety.'"

She left, but was with Jefferson when he was captured by Union troops, and spent the next two years of her life working for his release from prison. Jefferson was ultimately freed and they moved several times before his death in 1889. Gracious Varina, still unpopular in the South, then moved to New York and supported herself, until her death in 1906, by writing a variety of works, including a two-volume memoir on the life of her late husband.

MILITANT MARY

Mary Jackson just wanted a little food for her family. But that was hard to come by in the chaos of the war-torn Confederacy. So she decided to take matters into her own hands and organized a group of Richmond, Virginia, wives and mothers to protest at the Confederate capitol. Mary, outfitted with a six-gun and a knife, led over 1,000 hungry women on a rampage through the streets of Richmond in an event that marked the most significant domestic crisis to beset Jefferson Davis, who faced the women personally and offered them the money out of his own pockets. They were not appeased and Jefferson had to call in the city battalion to restore order.

Her Little Black Book

*W*hen all the dust had settled, the blood washed away, and the Civil War was beginning to fade into distant memory, one of the most powerful chronicles of that rending period turned out to be the diaries of **Mary Boykin Chestnut.** Born into a prominent South Carolina political family, she married John Chestnut, one of the largest landowners in the state, who would later serve at General P. G. T. Beauregard's and Confederate President Jefferson Davis' sides throughout the Civil War. Mary was the perfect Confederate officer's wife, elegantly serving as a shining example of the class and style that the bold officers who crowded into her drawing room were fighting to preserve.

In 1860, exiled to her family's Camden, South Carolina, estate, when her U.S. senator husband John resigned from the Senate and South Carolina seceded from the union in protest of Abraham Lincoln's election, Mary needed something to wile away the hours. So she took pen to hand and begin to compose her 400,000-word *Diary from Dixie*. In telling all, she seemed "fully prepared to send her spouse straight to the devil," notes Autumn Stephens in *Wild Women*. "'Oh, if I could put some of my reckless spirit into these discreet, cautious lazy men!'" she wrote.

"As the *Diary* made abundantly (though perhaps inadvertently) clear, Chestnut's desire to deposit John squarely in harm's way wasn't strictly a matter of politics. Having apparently graduated magna cum laude from the Strong and Silent school of masculine behavior, her husband 'could see me . . . hung, drawn, and quartered without moving a muscle,' complained the cantankerous chatterbox. Nor did he ever quite comprehend why Mary—like many erstwhile southern belles, a dyed-in-the-wool party animal— couldn't curb her rambunctious social life, let alone curtail periodic private opium binges. And on the topic of his relationship with a certain 'very haughty and highly painted dame,' he had absolutely nothing to say—other, of course, than to deny every-thing. ('What a credulous fool you must take me to be,' harped his helpmate.)

"John's militant Mrs., however, was completely capable of giving as good (or bad) as she got: when the ex-governor of South Carolina cast a lascivious look in her direc-tion, she boldly returned his smoldering gaze. 'I can make any body love me if I choose,' she boasted, and indeed, the passionate politico was soon her constant companion. Suffice it to say that this defensive offense had the desired effect. After a full week of fuming while his wife entertained 'the handsomest man on earth' under his own roof, laconic John finally let loose with a torrent of jealous invective. 'Is it not too funny,' chortled a greatly gratified Chestnut. 'He is so *prosy.*'

"Oddly enough, however, the warmongering wife was devastated when she realized in 1861 that John would soon see active duty. 'I feel he is my all and I should go mad without him,' she confessed to her *Diary*. That entry, however, was eventually erased; later readers could just make out the smudged lettering on the page, telltale evidence of the bedrock of love beneath the blazing matrimonial battlefield. On the domestic front as on the national, it seems, no warrior who hoped to survive could afford to wax senti-mental, nor to acknowledge her deep underlying kinship with the enemy."

> **❝**Does anybody wonder why so many women die? Grief and constant anxiety kill nearly as many women as men die on the battlefield.**❞**
> —*Mary Boykin Chestnut*

SIREN OF THE SHENANDOAH

*T*he most beautiful and notorious southern Civil War spy was **Belle Boyd,** the daughter of a tobacco plantation owner from Martinsburg, Virginia (now West Virginia). At sixteen, she had her first opportunity to show her loyalty to the Confederacy when, on July 4, 1861, a Union soldier entered her home and attempted to raise the Union flag. Her mother resisted; and, as the soldier began to manhandle her, Belle shot him dead. A year later, she was appointed to be a courier for Generals Beauregard and Jackson, using her good looks to move freely about and carry messages.

She was often found in the thick of battle and, in her autobiography, she describes one such occasion: "I soon cleared the town and gained the open fields . . . hoping to escape observation until such time as I could make my way to the Confederate line. . . . I had on a dark blue dress, with a little fancy white apron over it, and this contrast of colors, being visible at a great distance, made me far more conspicuous than was just then agreeable . . . the rifle-balls flew thick and fast about me, and more than one struck the ground so near my feet as to throw the dust in my eyes."

Fearless Belle, known now as the "Siren of the Shenandoah" for her notorious seduction of Union officers to gain information, is at least partially responsible for the 1862 Confederate victory at Fort Royal, Virginia. Familiar with the countryside, she personally pilfered Union sabers, pistols, and ammo, smuggling them to Rebel troops to help effect a victory. The North learned of her participation and arrested her on direct order of the Secretary of War. She was shipped off to Old Capitol Prison, but was released a month later in a prisoner swap, for she was causing too much trouble in prison, having already engineered the escape of three prisoners. A year later, she was arrested again and, having contracted typhoid fever in Old Capitol, was banished to the South.

However, Belle wasn't one to let a little case of typhoid stop her. Her next escapade was sailing on a blockade runner to England, carrying dispatches from Jefferson Davis to Confederate sympathizers in Europe. The ship was intercepted, Belle destroyed the letters, and the captain of the ship escaped while Belle distracted the arresting officer, Samuel Harding, whom she later married. But first it was off to prison again, this time in Boston. Trying desperately to get rid of her, Union officials decided to banish her to Canada this time. She went, but soon found her way to England again where she took up pen to scribe the two-volume, *Belle Boyd in Camp and Prison, Written by Herself*. She had been warned that her husband, who was imprisoned in Fort Delaware (presumably for Confederate sympathies), would be in danger if she published the book. She retaliated by threatening to expose Union atrocities if anything happened to him. Federal officials, deciding not to incur her wrath, sent him to reunite with her in England, where upon arrival he promptly died.

With the war over, Belle took up acting, making her American stage debut in 1868 and retiring a year later upon her marriage to English tea merchant John Hammond. She was twenty-four. The two were divorced after fifteen years (almost unheard of at that time). Belle, always a marriage-minded gal, promptly married Nat High, a man seventeen years her junior, and began acting again. She'd been busy in retirement, though. Not only did she have four children, but she evidently shot and wounded a young man who was courting her daughter and had refused to marry her. For the next fourteen years, until she died of a heart attack in 1900, she gave performances of *The Rebel Spy*, a dramatic narrative of her exploits during the Civil War. When she died, Union veterans, who remembered her fondly, carried her coffin—in true war hero style—to its final resting place.

CRAZY LIKE A FOX

Virginian **Mary Elizabeth Bowser** was born into slavery on a plantation outside of Richmond. Her emancipation came at the age of eighteen with the death of her owner John Van Lew, when his relative Elizabeth Van Lew freed all of his slaves. Moving North to pursue an education, Mary returned to Richmond at the outbreak of the Civil War to help Elizabeth, a white Union supporter also known as Crazy Bet, carry out acts of espionage under the guise of lunacy. Crazy Bet used Mary as a planted maid in the Confederate White House, where, in between dusting, she spied on President Jefferson Davis, peeked at documents, and reported back the insider information she unearthed. Like Bet, she pretended to be meek and crazy, and was never even suspected, but among her many tip offs was information that led to the fall of Richmond in 1864. Mary kept what is presumed to be a fascinating account of her spy work in the form of a diary, now in the private hands of a Richmond family that oddly has never allowed it to be publicly read.

The Wild Rose of the South

*R*ose O'Neal Greenhow was the widow of an attaché of the state department, a legendary beauty, and a gracious Washington, D.C., hostess who, "[l]ike every socialite worth her salted peanuts urged her guests to gossip. In contrast to D.C.'s fluffier femmes, however, Ms. Greenhow didn't have to feign fascination when cocktail chatter turned to military matters. A secret secessionist sympathizer, her aim was to extract every ounce of relevant information from her well-placed Union connections," writes Autumn Stephens in *Wild Women*. Her well-placed ear resulted in a number of Confederate victories, including the Battles of Manassas and Bull Run; the latter for which she had managed to send a ten-word message to General Beauregard that tipped him off as to what to expect from Union troops.

Trouble was, however, Union leaders knew where the leak was coming from and, in 1891, sent the famous detective Allen Pinkerton to arrest the delicate Rose. He placed her under house arrest while he conducted a thorough search, finding dozens of love letters and other incriminating evidence, some pieced together from the ashes discovered in the stove. When it became clear that Rose was still sending messages, she was sent to Old Capital Prison in Washington, D.C., where she continued her spying, sending encrypted messages in the buns of women visitors' hair; and, from her cell, she would wave a Confederate flag outside her window, crying "that no one could capture her soul," writes Stephens.

In 1862, after a number of well-placed lovers in D.C. clamored for mercy for her, Rose was released from prison and exiled to the Confederacy. There she received the thanks of Jefferson Davis—"But for you there would have been no Bull Run"—and $2,500 for her labors. But eventually life proved too tame for the Rebel madam so she ran the Union blockade along the southeastern seaboard to partake of a tour to Britain and France in order to raise funds and support for the Confederate cause. While in London, she wrote *My Imprisonment and the First Year of Abolitionist Rule in Washington*, which enjoyed brisk sales in Europe. The Europeans took to the author too, particularly the ruling class; and the secessionist spy was presented at court in both London and Paris (where she also received a private audience with Napoleon III). Soon Rose's pockets were bulging with cash for the Confederate cause; and, in 1864, she headed for home on the *Condor*, a British blockade runner. The *Condor* safely evaded the Union fleet, but ran aground at night on a sandbar near Fort Fisher, outside of Wilmington, North Carolina. Fearful of capture, Rose insisted upon being put ashore in a tiny row boat, despite the captain's warnings that the seas were too rough. The boat capsized. The men in the boat made it safely to shore; but Wild Rose drowned, reputedly dragged down by the weight of $2,000 in gold she carried in a heavy purse. She was buried with full military honors in the Oakdale Cemetery in Wilmington, her coffin draped with the Confederate flag; and she was carried to burial by Confederate troops.

66 I am a Southern woman, born with revolutionary blood in my veins. **99**
—*Rose O'Neal Greenhow*

THE SOIRÉE SISTERS

In 1863, **Celia and Winnie Mae Murphree** were babysitting in Blountsville, Alabama, when three Union soldiers stormed in, demanding medical supplies, fresh horses, and mint juleps. Celia and Winnie Mae dutifully prepared the drinks, but also mixed in a powerful sedative. The Yanks loved the drinks, ordered another round, and after quaffing the second, promptly passed out cold. The sisters then confiscated the men's weapons and turned them over to the Confederacy. Actually, without knowing it, Celia and Winnie Mae were following a tradition established long ago. Juleps, which are nothing more than sweet-tasting liquids, were used as early as the 17th century by pharmacists to disguise the taste of unpleasant medicine. *The Bartender's Bible* speculates that mint juleps were probably originally concocted to disguise the rough taste of whiskey before Kentucky (heavily debated by Tennessee) perfected a smooth bourbon. While mint juleps are traditionally served the first Saturday in May at the start of the Kentucky Derby, if you aren't a traditionalist, these delicious drinks, topped by fresh sprigs of mint, are the right thing to imbibe anytime you're in a "drankin' kinda" mood. Just don't be as heavy-handed as the Murphree sisters.

3

Shining Stars
and
Silver (Screen) Belles

The South is famous for its beautiful women and many of them have been able to parlay that God-given gift, along with a great deal of talent, into careers on stage and screen. Originally, it helped to be a blonde (natural or not); but the strength and emotional courage of several African American women have propelled them to beat the odds and score big too.

Hot-Blooded Hussy

The most outrageous actress on either side of the Mason-Dixon Line is undisputedly **Tallulah Bankhead.** With a career that spanned fifty years, she appeared in fifty-one plays, eighteen movies, and made countless radio, television and nightclub appearances; but she is best known for "molding her life into a stunning theatrical role," as *Notable American Women* puts it. Named for Tallulah Falls in her native Alabama, her throaty rasp, golden-blonde hair, ripping wit, and absolute scorn for convention conquered everybody she encountered in real life, on screen, and especially on stage where she triumphed brilliantly playing off her natural quick wit and sterling rapport with others. As Alfred Hitchcock, who directed her in the 1944 award-winning *Lifeboat,* put it, "The whole point about Tallulah was that she had no inhibitions." Scriptwriter Anita Loos said that no party was in full swing "until Tallulah arrived to put her particular type of zizz into it. She lived in the grand manner of a free soul with aristocratic disdain for caution." She also drank, swore like a sailor, took drugs, and was famous for her childish temper tantrums—always expecting to be treated like a well-bred southern lady, which she debatably was.

Nobody, past or present, could beat the stunning beauty, with the huge, expressive eyes, to a punch line. Born in 1902, the daughter of William Brockman Bankhead, who was speaker of the House of Representatives, and granddaughter of the famous Alabama Senator John Hollis Bankhead, Tallulah and her much-loved father both agreed that "If you know your Bible and your Shakespeare and can shoot craps, you have a liberal education."

Raised by her father (her mother died while giving birth to Tallulah) and not by wolves, as her wild reputation would have you believe, she was educated in a convent.

She sought fame in New York City, after winning a beauty contest at fifteen in Montgomery, Alabama. In 1923, she sailed to London and was a huge success in a variety of plays where she portrayed witty and daring women, dressed to the nines, attracting a huge following as a model for the "bright young things," the term used by the post-World War I generation determined to abandon the proprieties of the Victorian era. In the early 1930s, she headed to Hollywood where she made a series of semi-forgettable movies and lost the part of belle de jour, Scarlett O'Hara, in David O. Selznick's movie version of *Gone With the Wind*. She promptly returned to Broadway, where she triumphed as Regina in

Lillian Hellman's ruthless portrayal of the antebellum South, *The Little Foxes*, with 408 performances, and in 1942 as the temptress Sabina in *The Skin of Our Teeth*, with 359 performances, both roles garnering her the New York Drama Critics Circle awards for best actress.

She was famous for her sexual exploits with both men and women (including a rumored affair with actress Hattie McDaniel). Once, in Hollywood, she ran into former lover and swashbuckling actor, Douglas Fairbanks, Jr., and his new wife, Joan Crawford. In her whiskey voice, she said to Joan, "Dahling, you're divine. I've had an affair with your husband. You'll be next." Self-described as "pure as driven slush," in 1956, when asked by Tennessee Williams if she had ever had a lesbian relationship, she replied, "Yes, but that was in 1932, with Hope Williams, who had a boy's body." The next time she was impishly asked by the playwright, she replied that Eva Le Galliene had seduced her when she was sixteen; and Bankhead's much-quoted tirade against oral sex was "If you go down on a woman, you get a crick in the neck. If you go down on a man, you get lockjaw." She had a brief four-year marriage to actor John Emery in the '30s, but preferred her liaisons short and commitment free.

She was notorious for not wearing underwear on movie sets. In 1932, to shock people gaping at both her and actress Marlene Dietrich outside of their adjoining dressing rooms at Paramount studios, she took some of the gold dust that Dietrich wore in her hair, rubbed it on her pubic hair, and walked around exposing herself and crying, "Guess what I've been doing?"

The hot-blooded, ribald actress died in 1968 at age sixty-six, the latter years of her life spent doing largely camp versions of her own persona, including her role in the cult teleflick *Die, Die My Darling* with a young Stephanie Powers in 1963. A brilliant actress and icon, she has been embraced by hundreds of men and women for her no guts, no glory attitude and refusal to be anyone other than her own spectacular larger-than-life self.

"HELLO, DAAAAHLING": TALLULAH'S HOTTEST ONE LINERS

- When asked by famous sex researcher Alfred Kinsey to tell him about her sex life: "Of course, dahling, if you tell me about yours."

- "Nobody can be exactly like me. Sometimes even I have trouble doing it."

- "If I had my life to live over again, I'd make the same mistakes, only sooner."

- To a lover who didn't acknowledge her at a party, "What's the matter, dahling, don't you recognize me with my clothes on?"

- "Acting is a form of confusion."

- "My father warned me about men and booze, but he never said a word about women and cocaine."

- "Cocaine isn't habit-forming. I should know—I've been using it for years."

- "If you really want to help the American theater, don't be an actress, dahling. Be an audience."

- And to another eager lover, she exclaimed "I'll come and make love to you at five o'clock. If I'm late start without me."

Honorary Southerner

*T*he only African American woman to win an Oscar until Whoopi Goldberg's win for *Ghost* was **Hattie McDaniel,** as the best supporting actress for her role as Mammy in 1939's *Gone With the Wind.* Hattie, born the youngest of thirteen children of former slaves around 1895 in Kansas, actually lived in Denver most of her life, despite her public image as a "true" Southerner; she even had to teach herself a southern dialect for the screen. But she played the roles of southern maids so well, in so many movies, that everyone was convinced of a Dixie origin.

She got her start in vaudeville shows when she was fifteen, touring with her father and brothers. Later, she set out on her own to become a blues singer. She got gigs through the Theater Owners Booking Association (TOBA), which also jump-started stars such as Bessie Smith and Ida Cox. TOBA was famous for working singers hard and cheating them financially, which is why everyone on the circuit called it "Tough on Black Asses." TOBA went belly up during the Depression; and Hattie, after working a bit as a domestic, hightailed it to Hollywood.

All in all, she appeared in over sixty films, including *I'm No Angel, Alice Adams, Show Boat, Saratoga,* and many of the *Our Gang* shorts, becoming one of the best loved black performers at a time when whites monopolized the screen. She almost always played the same character—the only one written for black women at the time: a servile, but sassy maid who knew more than the white folks who employed (or owned) her. "Hattie McDaniel filled these roles with an ironic energy," claims *Notable American Women,* "using her massive figure, enormously mobile face, and rich voice to transform the meek servant into a knowing critic of the ways of the masters." According to *Black Women in America,* Hattie "began to find herself in competition with a small group of women who collectively portrayed all of Hollywood's mammies and maids. The group included Ethel Waters and Louise Beavers (who forced herself to overeat so that she would appear more mammy-like)."

Upon winning the Oscar, she began to promote herself as the character of Mammy, posing with mammy figurines and publishing recipes under Mammy's name. Despite the flack she took for perpetuating the stereotype of the hated Mammy figure, particularly from the NAACP, she was one of the founders of the Fair Play Committee, an organization that pushed for changes in the film industry such as discontinuing the use of the word "nigger." She often participated in fundraisers for scholarships for black children and waged a successful anti-discrimination legal battle over the purchase of her house in Los Angeles.

Because of the low wages she was paid, she never made much of a living from her screen work and did years of radio broadcasts on shows like *Amos and Andy* to help pay the rent. Married three times, she declared she was pregnant at age forty-nine and friends threw baby showers; when it was diagnosed as a false pregnancy, she fell into a deep depression and suffered from ill health from then on. After World War II, the market for comedic black maids dried up and the silver screen turned lily white. Hattie continued her radio work and tried her hand at television. She died at the Los Angeles Motion Picture Home and Hospital in 1952.

❝It's better to get $7,000 a week for playing a servant than $7 a week for being one.❞
—*Hattie McDaniel on why she played stereotyped domestics*

SHE'D HAD ENOUGH

Thelma "Butterfly" McQueen, the squeaky-voiced Prissy in *Gone With the Wind*, was famous in the 1940s for playing hysterically dimwitted domestics. But the Tampa, Florida, native had her limits—she refused to eat watermelon in the famous movie and only allowed herself to be slapped by Scarlett in the famous birthing scene after registering a protest. She retired from the movies in 1947 (though she did appear from time to time on television), because she resented playing the same stereotype over and over again, and held a number of menial jobs for twenty-five years. At the age of sixty-four, she graduated from college and went to work on behalf of Harlem school children.

Funny Gal

$\mathcal{Q}$uick-quipping comedian **Brett Butler** was supposed to have been born in Tuskegee, "only the hospital was in Montgomery, Alabama" she joked, but was raised in the great state of Georgia. Said the witty blonde (". . . Not!") in *The Comedy Magazine,* "I'm the type of southern Baptist that keeps a picture of Elvis' Last Supper in the living room. Whenever I mention that in my nightclub act, I usually get at least one irate Baptist who says, 'You can make fun of Jesus, but leave The King out of it!'"

She gets a lot of flack for her name, too. Many people think her parents were aiming for Scarlett's love interest or some sort of homage to *Gone With the Wind* (they weren't— they named her after Lady Brett Ashley in Ernest Hemingway's *The Sun Also Rises*); but she is also often confused with another famous B. B., male baseball player Brett Butler. She takes it in stride as fodder for her stand-up routines, which she has been performing since she was eight years old. After high school, she got married to an abusive man (as it turned out) and endured a painful three-year marriage before finding the gumption to get out of it. Alcohol was also involved; she once quipped, "My family is half Irish and half Swedish. They're all alcoholics, but we're real quiet about it."

Moving to Texas, she began to seriously cultivate her comedic talent, doing over 1,000 shows in two years. A female comic was a novelty in the South and audiences loved her honesty about her troubled life. But the bright lights of the big city proved too alluring; and so she got into her 1969 Grand Prix and drove to New York, where she proceeded to take the comedy club circuit by storm. In 1990, she was nominated for an American Comedy Award for funniest female stand-up. She now says she is "on [her] second marriage. You know, you let one guy get away, you're gonna have to build a taller fence and put better food out."

In 1993, she got the part of Grace Kelly, the lead in the television sitcom *Grace Under Fire,* whose character has a lot in common with Brett, although the show was created before she was actually cast. Her matter-of-fact style and great sense of timing has caught the attention of viewers. The first year, her show was in the top ten; the second year, in the top five. In 1997, she was also named executive producer. Its humor, as the following example demonstrates, is based in blue-collar fun: One day, Grace is playing in the traditionally all-male poker game with her refinery co-workers. When one makes a crack that women can't play cards because they can't bluff, she retorts, "Listen — if you can fake an orgasm, you can raise on a pair of twos."

66Politically, I'm a hypocrite. I'm a socialist with a Gold Card. I think we need a revolution, but I'm scared I won't be able to find any good moisturizer after it happens.99

—*Brett Butler*

"HOOWDEE!"

Minnie Pearl was the first successful Southern female stand-up comedian in the United States. Born Sarah Ophelia Colley in 1913, "she was a graduate of a fashionable finishing school, yet made her living portraying the hayseed spinster from Ginder's Switch," writes Bethany Bultman in *Redneck Heaven.* "One of her classic quotes regarding a wish for female pallbearers was, 'If those ol' boys won't take me out when I'm a-livin', I sure don't want 'em taking me out when I'm dead.'" The *Hee Haw* regular was rarely seen out of character, always wearing her straw boater with the price tag dangling down, until her death in 1996 at the age of eighty-three.

Boxed into a Corner

$\mathcal{S}$he had already been the Breck shampoo girl, a top model, and had appeared on *Charlie's Angels* and *The Six-Million Dollar Man*, but baring all at twenty for *Playboy* during the promotion of the James Bond flick, *Never Say Never Again*, helped put blonde bombshell **Kim Basinger** on the map and in the memories of thousands of male fans.

Beauty ran in the Athens, Georgia, native's family—Mom was a model. But fame was to be all Kim's own. Nicknamed "Dodo" by her four siblings when she was young,

she attended the University of Georgia and subsequently made a name for herself in the 1980s by having a purported affair with the musician Prince, shooting some steamy sex scenes with Mickey Rourke in *9½ Weeks*, and causing trouble on the set of *The Marrying Man* (where she met future husband Alec Baldwin). Several of her other films include *My Stepmother is an Alien, The Getaway, Blind Date, Nadine, Batman*, and *Ready to Wear*. Never one to shy away from controversy, rumors abound of the bad behavior on the part of both Kim and husband Alec Baldwin. As *Star Bios* points out, she and Alec celebrated the birth of their first child, daughter Ireland Eliesse, in October 1995, by having Alec punch out an intrusive photographer while bringing his daughter home from the hospital.

But the real controversy centers on poor Kim's money woes, which started in 1991, when she decided to pull out of the bizarre film, *Boxing Helena*. Not a bad artistic decision (the movie got uniformly panned), but an unwise financial one, it turns out. The thick-lipped beauty was sued by producer Carl Mazzocone, who, he claims, was only looking for "a simple apology and a phone call," as he told *People* magazine. Instead he ended up winning $8.9 million (later reduced to $3.8 million) from the actress. As a result, in 1993, she filed for bankruptcy and was forced to reveal her expenses item for item, exposing the fact that she spent $7,000 a month on pet care (she had seventeen dogs and cats) and other personal expenses, while an ex-husband of hers cost $9,000 a month in alimony. Kim also had to sell the town of Braselton, Georgia (population 418), which she bought in 1989 for $20 million, hoping to create a theme park, movie studios, housing, and shopping centers: selling price: $4.3 million.

But don't cry too hard for curvaceous Kim. She still has a great career and a handsome actor husband to pick up at least part of her tab. And if she takes after fellow Georgian and sister belle Scarlett at all, she, like the phoenix, will rise from the ashes once again.

66I don't have time to be classified as difficult and I don't have time to care.**99**
    —*Kim Basinger*

Red Hot "Moms"

*J*ackie **"Moms" Mabley** was a salty comedian best known for her stand-up skits as a gravelly-voiced "dirty old lady." She patterned the character after her grandmother, a former slave who lived to be over one hundred years old.

Like many comedians, Moms had a hard life, but it never showed on stage. Born Loretta Mary Aiken in 1897 in Brevard, North Carolina, she was one of seven children. Her father died in an accident as a volunteer fireman when she was very young; and her stepfather beat her. At age eleven, she was raped by a black man and at age thirteen, by a white man. By fourteen, she had two children. Her grandmother told her to run away from home if she ever wanted to be somebody, so she did. Claiming to be sixteen, she joined a minstrel show and hooked up with Jack Mabley. The duo never married, but she took his name because, she often said, "He took so much off a' me, the least I could do was take his name."

She began to tour the network of African American clubs throughout the South and worked in African American theater, sometimes appearing in blackface. During the Harlem Renaissance of the 1920s, she went off the "chitlin circuit," appearing instead in nightclubs along with Cab Calloway, Duke Ellington, Count Basie, and Louis Armstrong. "Later she created comedy routines from her encounters and supposed love affairs with these immortals of entertainment," notes *Black Women in America*. She became a regular at the famed Apollo in Harlem; and hers was the longest running act in the theater's history. And she even did a Broadway production in which she collaborated with Zora Neale Hurston, the two appearing together as cheerleaders. In the '30s, she appeared in her first film, *The Emperor Jones*, and played Quince in a jazz adaptation of *A Midsummer Night's Dream*, subsequently adding satire of the classics to her routine. Then, in 1948, she played the lead role of Moms in *Boarding House,* the character she was to cultivate to perfection: huge roving eyes, a baggy dress, sloppy hat, loose stockings, few teeth, and too big shoes, with a taste for younger men and language like a sailor.

She'd been given the nickname Moms by fellow show people whom she had cared for; but she soon realized that it worked well on stage. In taking on the persona of Moms, explains *Black Women in America,* she was following in the footsteps of many women for whom the tactic had been effective: Ma Rainey, Sweet Mama Stringbean (Ethel Waters), and The Last of the Red Hot Mamas were just three of the entertainers who sought protection from accusations of immorality under the cloak of motherhood. Over the decades, Moms developed her character fully, passing out folk wisdom along with the jokes, advising presidents (John F. Kennedy invited her to the White House) and flattening racists.

The character stood her in good stead throughout the rest of her life. She easily adapted to television, appearing regularly on *The Smothers Brothers Comedy Hour, The Ed Sullivan Show, The Merv Griffin Show,* and *The Flip Wilson Show.* Her album, *Moms Mabley: The Funniest Woman in the World* sold over one million copies. During the filming of the movie *Amazing Grace* in 1975, in which she starred as a little old lady who tackled big criminals, she had a heart attack and died shortly after it was completed.

❝Love is like playing checkers. You have to know which man to move.**❞**
—Jackie "Moms" Mabley

In Jacy's Shadow

Cybill Shepherd's been up and she's been down; but she's always been forthright about herself. A world famous cover girl by the age of eighteen—she only took up modeling "to get out of Memphis," she claims, bursting onto the movie scene at age twenty-one in the unforgettable *The Last Picture Show* as the predatory Jacy Farrow. She was

afraid of doing the part for fear that audiences would think that the character was her; and, for years after, she was seen as a manipulative, cold creature.

But the former Miss Congeniality at the Miss Teenage America Pageant maintains it just ain't so, although rumors continued to fly during the '80s when she starred in the television hit *Moonlighting* with Bruce Willis. "Willis and I used to fight about hair," she once told writer Darcy Rice in an interview, "He just hated my hairstyle. He would go to my hairdresser and say, 'It's so old-fashioned, can't you do something that's more modern?' I would get so irritated with him that I would snit back: 'At least I have hair.'"

She hit a dry spell professionally both before and after *Moonlighting* (though she did appear in several other movies including Scorsese's masterpiece *Taxi Driver* and has done lengthy stints as a

WINNING MISS FROM OLE MISS

Mary Ann Mobley is another southern beauty pageant winner turned actress. Born in 1939 in Brandon, Mississippi, she dreamt of becoming a missionary. But in 1956, Bing Crosby picked her as the winner of the Ole Miss Parade of Beauties and her career as a pageant queen was launched. In 1959, the future Mrs. Gary Collins became Miss America. And from there it was on to Broadway, off-Broadway, movies and television, appearing with Elvis in *Girl Happy* and as a regular on *Diff'rent Strokes,* where she played the white rebel belle surrogate mother of two black children.

torch singer); but the determined belle made yet another comeback in the 1990s, this time as a struggling actress (sound familiar?) on television's *Cybill.* The show deals humorously, but truthfully, about an (albeit beautiful) fortysomething woman's dating problems, menopause symptoms, struggles with ex's, best friends, children moving back home, and the dilemma of facelifts (so far the character and the actress have both said no to the last item).

The forty-seven-year-old comedian, whose southern accent still comes through from time to time on her show, considers it important that viewers see her natural (non-lifted) face and refuses to lie about her age. She maintains this is a personal tradition that began when *Last Picture Show* director (at the time her very married lover), Peter Bogdanovich, asked her at age twenty-one to lie and say she was seventeen. She emphatically said no because it was "boring . . . to keep track of that lie." While making no promises to never have cosmetic surgery, she does declare, "From a very early age I helped propagate the whole beauty myth, the drive toward this perfection, this impossible ideal, that young women are crippled by. I think our society is insane, our worship of youth. I have an obligation to tell the truth about what I am going through."

66 I just refuse to give up longer than a couple of weeks. **99**
— *Cybill Shepherd*

ONE LUCKY MISS

Cheryl Prewitt was in a car accident in 1968 and, as a result, her left leg was shorter than the right. But at a revival in Jackson, Mississippi, in 1974, three hundred people prayed over her leg, and right in front of her very eyes, as she later told the *New York Times*, "I sat there and watched my leg grow out instantaneously two inches." We know of this miracle because she went on to become Miss America in 1980. Speaking of Miss America, if you want to become one, it would behoove you to study up on being a southern belle (rumor has it the typical belle is the judges' operating standard) or simply attend the University of Mississippi—known as Ole Miss—which has produced three reigning queens: Mary Ann Mobley, Lynda Meade, and Susan Atkin.

THE MOST BEAUTIFUL GIRL IN THE WORLD

Born on a tobacco farm in Grabtown, North Carolina, **Ava Gardner** is one of the most glamorous movie stars of all time, although she never lost her love of earthy language and going barefoot, which she claims comes from growing up in the rural South. She was the youngest of seven children, born on Christmas Eve, 1922, into a poor family that didn't put a premium on education. By the time she was twenty-four, she maintained, she had read only two books: the Bible and *Gone With the Wind*. As an adult, however, she became a voracious autodidact.

Hers is a fairy tale story. When she was eighteen, an MGM scout saw a photo of her in the window of her brother-in-law's photography studio in New York City and, based on her extraordinary beauty (many people still claim she was the most beautiful actress in film history), signed her to a contract. For her first seventeen roles, she had little more than one line parts, but eventually she made her way to her first starring role in *Whistle Stop*. In 1946, MGM loaned her out for *The Killers*, which is thought to be one of her best roles. (It is also the only movie that features her singing; much to her chagrin, in all her movies for MGM, her singing was dubbed.)

In general, MGM, which kept her under contract for seventeen years, cast her in only mediocre movies, capitalizing on her fame and beauty to sell tickets. Ava was nonplussed, saying, "I have only one rule in acting—trust the director and give him heart and soul." She made sixty-one movies; notable among them are *Mogambo* with Clark Gable in 1956, *The Night of the Iguana* in 1964, and *The Barefoot Contessa* in 1954, for which she learned flamenco. Flamenco ultimately became one of the tempestuous actress' favorite pastimes; it's a good thing she needed little sleep, for she was famous for dancing all night. "I must have seen more sunrises than any other actress in the history

of Hollywood," she once quipped.

She had three famous husbands, all of whom she remained friends with. The first was actor and child star, Mickey Rooney; their marriage lasted sixteen months. Her next marriage to the famous band leader, Artie Shaw, lasted only one year. But then there was Frank Sinatra. The two, widely believed to be the great love of one another's lives (they recently were named by *People* magazine as one of the great romances of the century), were married for nine years, but ultimately could not survive their jealousy of one another.

After their divorce, Ava moved to Spain, where she became an avid bullfighting fan. Later she moved to London, where she spent her last twenty-two years, coming to the U.S. to make a few movies, "strictly for the loot." One such trip produced the terrible 1970s disaster flick *Earthquake* in Sensaround—a theatrical gimic that made the theater shake along with the movie. Ava had little respect for acting—"nobody ever called it an intellectual profession" and once summed up her life thusly: "I haven't taken an overdose of sleeping pills and called my agent. I haven't been in jail, and I don't go running to the psychiatrist every two minutes. That's something of an accomplishment these days."

The raven-haired beauty remains beloved even after her death, with thirteen biographies to her name. There's even an Ava Gardner museum in Smithfield, North Carolina, started by Tom Banks, who at the age of twelve was kissed on the cheek by a young girl in Wilson, North Carolina. Two years later, Tom opened a newspaper and discovered through a photo that the girl was none other than Ava. When he grew up, he and his wife collected Ava memorabilia and, in the 1980s, he purchased the house she had lived in from age twelve to thirteen and operated a museum there until his death. His wife then donated the collection to the Town of Smithfield. In the first nine months of 1996, the museum had over 1,300 visitors; and its website page logs 700 visitors per month.

> **66** When I lose my temper, honey, you can't find it anyplace. **99**
> —*Ava Gardner*

THAT MERKEL WOMAN

Una Merkel began her film career as a stand-in for Lillian Gish; but soon her comic potential was discovered and she appeared in ninety-five films, between 1923 and 1966. The Covington, Kentucky, gal with peroxide blonde hair and the smooth as silk southern accent usually played the heroine's no-nonsense friend. Nominated for best supporting actress in *Summer and Smoke,* she is best known for her hair-pulling fight with über-actress Marlene Dietrich in *Destry Rides Again.*

OTHER SOUTHERN BELLES (AND TWO FAUX) OF THE SMALL AND LARGE SCREEN

True Belles

Kate Jackson: Birmingham, Alabama
Julia Roberts: Smyrna, Georgia
Holly Hunter: Conyers, Georgia
Kathy Bates: Memphis, Tennessee
Courtney Cox: Birmingham, Alabama
Carol Burnett: San Antonio, Texas
Dixie Carter: McLemoresville, Tennessee
Annie Potts: Franklin, Kentucky

Faux Belles

Jean Smart: Seattle, Washington,
the only non-Southerner on *Designing Women*

Rue McClanahan: Healdton, Oklahoma,
the oversexed belle on *The Golden Girls*

The Pride Of Kosciusko

$\mathcal{T}$here is no doubt that the most popular star from the South these days is talk-show queen, actress, and entertainment mogul, **Oprah Winfrey.** Born in Kosciusko, Mississippi, in 1954, the result of, as she puts it, "a one-day fling under an oak tree," she was to have been named for Orpah, the Biblical sister of Ruth, but someone got the spelling wrong. Left with her maternal grandmother and grandfather, Oprah's mother, Vernita Lee, went north, seeking better work than was available to her in Mississippi.

The future world-famous face had quite a brain attached. She could read by the age of three and, by six, had advanced to the third grade. That's when she went to live with her mother in Milwaukee and life turned into a nightmare. Her mother, an overworked domestic, was often away from home; and, from the age of nine to twelve, Oprah was sexually abused by several men. She began to act out, doing poorly in school and running away from home; and in desperation, her mother sent her to live with her father in Nashville.

It turned out to be a lucky move. Under the stern protection of her father, she began to do well in school again, getting a job as a local radio news broadcaster and winning a scholarship to Tennessee State University in an Elks Club oratory contest. While a freshman at TSU, she won the Miss Black Nashville and Miss Black Tennessee titles and was a contestant in the Miss Black America contest. This led to a job as Nashville's first woman television co-anchor, while she was still in college. Just a few months shy of graduation, she was lured away by a job at an ABC network affiliate in Baltimore. (In 1988, the university would give her a diploma based on her accomplishments; and she, in turn, created a scholarship fund for ten students a year.)

As time went on, she began to co-host the morning talk show, a job she would hold for seven years, before moving to Chicago to take over *AM-Chicago*, which was floundering in the ratings against local favorite, Phil Donahue. A month later, Oprah was neck-and-neck with Phil; and a year and a half later, it became *The Oprah Winfrey Show*. By 1986, the show went national (in a syndication deal that was reputed to have been for $30 million, making Oprah the highest paid performer in show business), ultimately running Phil off the airwaves altogether.

But she's not just all talk. In 1985, she starred as Sophia in *The Color Purple,* which landed her an Academy Award nomination. In 1989, she produced the miniseries, *The Women of Brewster Place;* and her production company owns the rights to many other projects, including Toni Morrison's novel, *Beloved.* However, with 15–20 million viewers and with an enormous twenty-five Emmys to its credit, the show, now simply called *Oprah,* is clearly her main focus. She's recently tackled more serious subjects in non-sensational ways and instituted Oprah's Book Club, which booksellers are crediting with creating new readers and saving literary fiction.

The key to her popularity? There has been endless speculation in the press, but thinking fast on her feet, combined with a willingness

to be open about her own life, including her weight struggles and sexual abuse, makes her someone that her mostly female, mostly young audience, can relate to. There's no doubt she is a powerful and positive role model for girls and women throughout the country.

> **❝**I want to be able to spread the message that you are responsible for your life and to set up a format to teach people how to do that.**❞**
> —*Oprah Winfrey*

AMERICA'S SELF-DUBBED BLACK SEX KITT

That's none other than **Eartha Kitt,** the sultry entertainer best known for her sexily ironic performances as Catwoman on television's 1967 *Batman*—when, by the way, she was already forty years old. A singer (she recorded the original "Santa Baby," in 1953), dancer, and actress from South Carolina, where she was raised by foster parents, she was famous for playing the edge between sex kitten and uppity woman. But she went over the top in 1968. Invited to the White House by Lady Bird Johnson with fifty other people to discuss urban crime, she was supposed to make nice. Instead she made trouble, speaking out against the Vietnam War: "You send the best of this country off to be shot and maimed." The incident caused investigations by both the CIA and FBI; and she has worked primarily in Europe ever since, although she appeared in Carnegie Hall in 1985 and her album, *I Love Men,* was a popular disco anthem in the 1980s.

LADY JANE

OK, so she is only a Southerner by marriage. But **Jane Fonda,** dubbed "Jane of a Thousand Faces" by *Atlanta* magazine — "who has had as many distinct lives as Madonna" as *Vanity Fair* opines — is really giving it the old southern try. The Barbarella, turned Vietnam protester, turned left-wing activist, turned fitness "go for the burn" queen, turned Ted Turner's wife is doing a good job in her latest incarnation. You can see her with her "swatch of goldish hair that corresponded to no known color in nature," as Barbara Grizzuti Harrison so deftly put it in *The New York Times Magazine,* in Atlanta, at Braves games (husband Ted owns the team), cheerily doing the (very politically incorrect) tomahawk chop. And rumor has it that, when she wed Ted, she agreed to never spend even a single night away from his side (days apparently are left up to her). Will the South hold her heart forever? Or will the 21st century usher in yet another renewed and remade Jane? Stay tuned . . .

Out of the Mouths of Belles

66 When I'm asked why Southern writers particularly have a penchant for writing about freaks, I say it's because we are still able to recognize one. 99

— *Flannery O'Connor*

66 I'm not crazy, I've just been in a very bad mood for the last 40 years! 99

— *Shirley MacLaine as Ouiser Boudreaux,* Steel Magnolias

66 I'm not much of a Southern belle. Southern women tend to be real demure. They don't like to talk about anything graphic. I had a girl-friend who told me she was in the hospital for female problems. I said, 'Get real! What does that mean?' She says, 'You know, female problems.' I said, 'What, you can't parallel park? You can't get credit?' 99

— *Pam Stone*

66 I don't want to live — I want to love first, and live incidentally. 99

— *Zelda Fitzgerald*

66 As a woman, I find it very embarrassing to be in a meeting and realize I'm the only one in the room with balls. 99

—*Rita Mae Brown*

66 What a letdown. I think I'm going to be a Southern belle and I get sold down the river. 99

—*Chiquita Hart in* Something for the Boys *(1944)*

66 I have learned in the great University of Hard Knocks a philosophy that no woman who has had an easy life ever acquires. I have learned to live each day as it comes, and not to borrow trouble by dreading tomorrow. It is the dark menace of the future that makes cowards of us. 99

—*Dorothy Dix*

66 Well, I certainly don't believe God's a woman, because if He were, men would be the ones walking around wearing high heels, taking Midol, and having their upper lips waxed. 99

—*Dixie Carter,* Designing Women

4

Politicos in Petticoats

Republican, Democrat, Dixiecrat, Reform, Independent Peoples, Communist, Green—no matter what party you choose, politics in the South, and politics involving Southerners, is one of the most interesting and colorful, if not more outrageous, arenas for public speculation, opinion, controversy, and chaos. From the promotion of inept and inexperienced buffoons to heads of state, and puppet leaderships controlled vicariously by strippers, land barons, and certain demographic groupings, in southern politics there are no sacred cows and anything goes. Why, in the state of Alabama alone, the position of governor in the last thirty years has been held by a former vacuum cleaner salesman and convicted felon (Guy Hunt), a man who rode the coattails of his political first wife, a former governor herself, back into office (the beloved Lurleen and the heavily debated George Wallace), and the present Republican governor (Forrest "Fob" James), who had previously held the same office as a Democrat almost twenty years before!

TELL MA YOUR TROUBLES

Ma **Ferguson** could have only happened in Texas. Nowhere else could you find the fertile ground for political courage, corruption, and bizarre contradictions that characterized the twenty-year span of Fergusonism. In the early days of her marriage, Ma Ferguson (the "Ma" was a lazy Texas journalist's fortuitous abbreviation of Miriam Amanda) was content to play the role of the good southern politician's wife—that is, to smile sweetly and tend to the kids. In fact, her major accomplishment as the First Lady of Texas during husband Jim's first stint as governor was the construction of a greenhouse.

Then came the second term. Jim (Pa) Ferguson was hardily reelected in 1916; but, by the end of 1917, his political career came to a screeching halt. After leaving himself open for a fight with the University of Texas by vetoing certain appropriations for the school, he found himself on the losing end of impeachment proceedings for financial mismanagement. Since "financial finagling" was a long-time Texas tradition and Pa was the only Texas governor ever impeached, the sting of disgrace and unfairness cut deep into Ma's soul.

Subsequently, Pa spent seven long years in a misguided attempt to get the Texas courts to right this peculiar wrong; but, when all else seemed to fail, he came up with a great idea. In 1924, Pa, an ardent (and fortunately losing) opponent of women's suffrage, announced that his wife was running for governor, thus beginning the curious southern tradition of putting forward women as politicians by proxy. Running on a campaign slogan "Two Governors for the Price of One"—a slogan considered stunningly accurate in hindsight—Ma swept into office by pleading with the newly enfranchised women voters of Texas to "help me clear my family name!" Ma just missed being the first women governor in the country, however, by fifteen days; she was elected the same day as Nellie Tayloe Ross of Wyoming, but the Westerners moved faster in the swearing-in.

But family politics weren't all the Fergusons were about. "Po' folk populists," who seemed at least to feel for the common man (and then woman), Ma and Pa were ardent enemies of the Klu Klux Klan, seriously divided on prohibition (he was against it/she was for it), and united in their call for penitentiary reform. In her first term—where she was largely viewed as a figurehead—she passed anti-mask legislation and managed to argue for tougher prohibition-enforcement laws. She also pardoned scores of prisoners, many victims of an antiquated old west prison system, but many more beneficiaries of Pa Ferguson's "Cash and Carry" parole system where, for a price, prisoners could purchase their release. Most of the remaining term was wasted on an unsuccessful attempt

LEARNING THE HARD WAY

An interesting side note to the Ferguson reign is that Lyndon Baines Johnson apparently learned—painfully—everything he knew about manufacturing ballots from Pa Ferguson, who engineered LBJ's only electoral defeat in the special Senate race of 1941. It seems Pa wanted to get the irritating Pappy O'Daniel out of Texas and to help elect Coke Stevenson governor. Things came full circle when Pa died without ever having received as much as a cursory "thank you" call from Stevenson. Ma, never one to forget or forgive, swung her support back to LBJ in 1948 and set him on a course that would eventually take him to the White House.

to reinstate Pa's (then the governor-appointed highway commissioner in charge of the single largest pot of money flowing through Texas) electoral rights of office, which he had lost with his impeachment.

Ma, however, lost the next two Democratic primaries she entered, but reappeared in 1932 for still another try. This time she won again by a significant margin—though many claimed that more people had voted for her than were eligible to vote (perhaps the start of another fine, old Texas tradition). Ma's second administration was reputed to be more her own—she distanced herself some from Pa and attached herself firmly to Franklin Delano Roosevelt's New Deal, managing to alleviate the worst suffering for many Texans during the Depression. Pa, in the meantime, appears to have been preoccupied with selling pardons as a part of the new prison reform.

66 Southerners will forgive anybody anything if they have good manners. Once a particularly charming Congressman who had been a guest at a church dinner my mother had attended was caught sometime later rather, well, flagrantly, as the French would say, in a motel room wearing a dog collar and his wife's lace bra and panties. Mother's response when asked if she would vote for him again? 'Why, of course. After all, everybody's got their little quirks. Besides he has lovely table manners.' **99**

—*Fannie Flagg*

THE MOUTH THAT ROARED

*M*artha **Elizabeth Beall Jennings Mitchell,** widely known as "Martha the Mouth," was one of the most controversial figures of her time. The Arkansas native once claimed that "I would have been alright if I'd never left the South," and she may have been right, since the South, at least, had a long tradition of taking in stride strong women who operated like loose cannons on automatic.

Martha's woes began when, in a second marriage, she tied the knot with Richard Nixon's close friend and future campaign manager/Attorney General, John Mitchell. Pleased as punch by the important political company she was keeping (except for her nagging fear that Nixon was too liberal), Martha suddenly found that reporters would listen to anything she said, so she said anything that came to mind. Once she told a reporter that her dear Attorney General hubby often claimed he'd love to trade some of our liberals for some Russian communist. And when a visitor to a White House event spoke out against the Vietnam War, Martha made one of her soon-to-be famous late night calls to a reporter and insisted that the woman should be "torn limb-from-limb."

But if Martha's mouth appalled the Democrats, it horrified the president and his merry band of men. Nixon used to plead with John to control her; but he just threw up his hands, professed his love, and claimed she was "an unguided missile." However, Martha's missile didn't miss her main target, once she realized that her husband was being set up to take the fall for Watergate. In one late night flurry of calls, when the man known as Tricky Dick was trying to distance himself from John by insisting he hadn't met with him, Martha told half the reporters on the eastern seaboard that Nixon's comment was a "God-blessed lie." When the attorney general was indicted on charges of interfering with the Watergate investigation, Martha called up one of her favorite reporters, Helen Thomas, and said, "I'll be damned if I'll let my husband take the rap for Mr. President. If my husband knew anything . . . Mr. Nixon also knew about it."

But while Martha was ratting out the president in grand style, nobody was taking her seriously; conservatives were angry that she was attacking the chief and she had irritated those on the left so much so that there was no one who would come to her defense. The full implications of Watergate had yet to surface; and Martha's mouth had already destroyed much of her own credibility. As the Watergate hearings heated up, so too did the heat on Martha. At one point, she called Helen Thomas and claimed that, not only was she under constant surveillance, but that five men from the Committee to Re-elect the President had broken into the motel she was staying in, ripped the phone out of the wall, drugged, and beat her: "I'm black and blue, I'm a political prisoner," she lamented. Still, "Martha stories" were regularly written almost as humor pieces, often with an angle of the tragic doings of a woman gone wrong.

Eventually even John Mitchell (who served time in a country club-style minimum security prison) abandoned her; and she died from cancer in 1976, after a long battle with alcohol and prescription drug abuse. It wasn't until years after Martha faded from the headlines that it became clear that much of what she had claimed had been true. For a few years, you could even spot cars driving around the country with the bumper sticker "Martha: You were Right!"

The final insult came after her death, when Nixon himself tried to shift much of the blame for Watergate onto Martha, by claiming that, if John Mitchell had not had to spend so much energy trying to keep her in line, he would have made sure that the Watergate break-in never happened. Don't you just wonder what Martha would have said to that?

THE BELLE OF ASHBY STREET

*H*elen **Douglas Mankin** was no deferential belle. Without bothering to go much out of her way she managed to scandalize, excite, and ruffle the feathers of most of traditional Georgian society. But then she came from serious contrarian stock—her parents met at the law school they both attended in 1887, even though her mother was prevented from practicing in Georgia by the genteel "rule" that deemed law an unfit endeavor for a young lady.

In 1918, after graduating from college, Helen put her own spin on the "acceptable" pursuit of a nursing career by taking off to Europe and driving ambulances for an American hospital unit working with the French Army. Post-war, she returned to Atlanta and promptly earned her law degree from the Atlanta law school started years before by her father. By then, the sensibility of the Georgian bar towards women lawyers had changed; and both mother and daughter were admitted to the bar in 1920.

Two years later, fed up with the treatment she received from her male colleagues, Helen decided to put the automotive skill she learned on the battlefields of Europe to good use. She and her sister Jean took off on a record-setting 13,000 mile grand tour of North America, sending back daily dispatches to the *Atlanta Georgian*.

After returning to Atlanta, she met and married Guy Mankin, a globe-trotting engineer; and Helen spent the next few years whirling through Cuba, Argentina, and Brazil, finally returning to Atlanta in 1933. By now, somewhat of an exotic local character, Helen successfully ran for state representative from Fulton County after getting fed up with the legislature's unwillingness to ratify a child labor amendment to the U.S. Constitution. While campaigning, she did a fine job of irritating the conservative political establishment led by Governor Eugene Talmadge by fighting for such radical things as child welfare, education reform, women's rights, and electoral reform.

At that time, Georgia had an "all-white" primary system (which was currently under fire at the Supreme Court) so, when a special election was called in 1946 to fill the recently vacated Fifth District seat, Helen jumped into the race and won—largely by the massive voting support from the black Ashby Street section of Atlanta. Such "pandering to the black vote" made Governor Talmadge spitting mad—he called Helen "the Belle of Ashby Street" and she proudly accepted the title.

Helen beat her opponent later that year in the "all-white" primary by 10,000 votes; but Governor Talmadge and the political establishment would exact their revenge by dusting off a little-used electoral counting system that weighted votes by county in order to "counterbalance" the black vote. To its shame, the U.S. Supreme Court upheld the bizarre counting method and the practice—which had gained great popularity in many parts of the South—and it wasn't tossed out until 1962.

While the case was being decided, Helen Mankin served in Congress; but her term lasted less than a year. During that time, she put herself to good use, further irritating the southern political establishment by supporting Harry Truman's veto of the anti-strike bill. The South, which was extremely anti-labor, didn't like the idea of workers having the ability to walk out. "Too bad," said righteous Helen.

❝ In Texas, politics is a contact sport. **❞**
  —*Ann Richards*

BULLISH BELLE

*T*he debate over the boundaries of "The South" has gone on for over 150 years; but, when the securely Southern of the deep South are asked about Texas, a common response is, "Texas, now that's something else entirely." This is perhaps the perfect description of **Barbara Jordan,** the black congresswoman from Houston with the voice that could rattle windows and souls. Barbara was indeed something else entirely.

In a state whose legislature was defined by the good-ol'-boy network, this larger than life (literally) woman was elected in 1966 to the Texas State Senate—not the lower house where she lost two elections, but *the Senate*, the inner sanctum of the good ol' boys. Needless to say, she was not welcomed with open arms. Some of her colleagues used to invite drinking buddies up to the gallery to make fun of the "nigger" when she spoke. You can imagine how long that lasted, by listening in your mind to the largely illiterate, mean-spirited razing from the gallery, being run over by Barbara's intensely precise logic delivered in her extraordinary booming bass voice that could literally captivate an entire auditorium. By the end of her first term, the hecklers were silenced; and she had won over her colleagues so thoroughly that she was the first freshman senator ever appointed to the Texas Legislative Council.

Her six-year term in the Texas State Senate is still talked about with awe. Not only did she tear down the doors that had previously held back so many women and African Americans, but she proved to be a relentlessly fine legislator, out horse-trading the very best of them, out smarting the lot of them, and gaining so much respect in the process that in 1972, her last year in the Texas Legislature, Barbara Jordan was unanimously elected as the president pro tempore.

Later that same year, she ran for U.S. Congress in a newly redrawn district she had

wrangled out of LBJ and the power brokers of the Texas Democratic party, becoming the first African American woman from the South to enter the halls of Congress. Once again, Barbara Jordan wowed them with her razor-sharp mind and incalculably immense personal presence. Within two years, the rest of the country would get the opportunity to witness what Texans already knew, when Barbara was appointed to Peter Rodino's House Judiciary Committee and single-voicedly dominated the nationally-televised impeachment hearings of Richard Nixon. After stating her intention to vote for impeachment, she seemed to stare out through the television cameras across the face of the entire nation and uttered the phrase that to this day sums up that entire period: "My faith in the Constitution is whole, it is complete, it is total." Each syllable articulated, boomed out across the country in a voice that made you catch your breath. The woman was an almighty presence of calm and security.

Born in Houston, in the heart of black Texas, to a Baptist minister and his wife, Barbara decided early on she was going to make something of herself using education as her ticket. She graduated magna cum laude from Texas Southern University, got her law degree from Boston University, and brought them both back to the Fifth Ward of Houston. So high did Barbara Jordan rise that she was chosen to be the keynote speaker for the 1976 Democratic Convention. So clear was her vision that she refused to be pressured into running for the vice-presidential nomination that year, telling all who would listen that America was not ready for a black woman a heart-beat away from the presidency.

To the shock and surprise of many, Barbara Jordan, regularly appearing in opinion polls as one of the ten most influential members of Congress, retired from Congress in 1978. Shortly afterwards, she developed multiple sclerosis. She spent the last years of her life, many of them from a wheelchair, inspiring students at the School of Public Affairs at the University of Texas and providing counsel to the next generation of public servants. Barbara Jordan was a belle with the strength of ten bulls, who changed the world, never taking "no" for an answer.

SOCIAL SEPTUAGENARIAN

*I*n the world of national contributions by southern political women, **Lillian Carter,** the mother behind her presidential boy, has had more lasting positive influence than her "mama's" role would suggest. Miz Lillian inherited a strong sense of compassion and a thirst for social justice from her postmaster father, James Jackson, who used to turn his Richland, Georgia, post office into an impromptu dining hall for traveling African Americans who could not get served at the local hotel.

Born in the waning years of the 19th century, Lillian lived a life that brought together the unusual, yet powerful, combination of hard-nosed political activism and deeply rooted moral integrity. In 1923, at age twenty-five, the feisty Lillian Jackson married James Earl Carter, a marriage that would last thirty years until his death in 1953. In quick order, the now famous Carter brood, including two boys, James Earl, Jr.

(Jimmy) and William Alton (Billy, famous for the beer bearing his moniker), acting as bookends for sisters Gloria and Ruth (close friend of *Hustler* publisher Larry Flynt), arrived, completing the family structure that would be Lillian's overriding concern for the rest of her life. But while Lillian's dedication and allegiance to her family was legendary, it was not unaccompanied by a wry sense of humor. Late in life, long after Jimmy had "lusted in his heart" and Billy had publicly embarrassed

himself for the umpteenth time, Lillian commented "I love all my children, but some of them I don't like." Once she even opined, in her most quoted remark, "Sometimes when I look at my children I say to myself, 'Lillian, you should have stayed a virgin.'"

Having worked as a nurse in Plains, Georgia, during the early years of her marriage, Miz Lillian helped run her husband's peanut farm, and provided the sage political sounding board and in-the-trenches campaigning to get him elected (and respected) as a member of the Georgia state legislature. When he died in 1953, the Democratic party offered Lillian his seat; but at the time she was too overwhelmed by sorrow to throw herself into her own political career. It was what many observers view in hindsight as one of those decisive turning points of her life. There is little doubt that Lillian Carter had the right stuff—and the right connections—to rise in political circles; but she chose instead to turn, in that time of sorrow, to the tending and healing of her family.

Lillian's political bent and moral stance, however, had plenty of opportunity to flourish in the brewing battle over civil rights and in her son's budding political career. As a homegrown figure of enormous respect and later as a leader in the Democratic party's civil rights efforts in Georgia, she typified the best aspects of southern dignity by playing a pivotal role in steering the state through the worst of those troubled times with a minimum rending of the social fabric. When son Jimmy proclaimed the "end to racial discrimination in Georgia" at his inaugural address as Governor of Georgia in 1970, Lillian Jackson Carter's voice could be heard ringing loud and clear. But managing a farm, campaigning for civil rights, and raising a president wasn't enough for this indefatigable campaigner; so in 1966, at the age of sixty-seven, she took off for a two-year stint in India with the Peace Corps.

A self-proclaimed "simple small town girl" who liked bourbon and hated to get all dressed up, Lillian Carter died in 1983 at the age of eighty-five; but her legacy lives on.

It flourishes in the memory of that powerful conscience that helped bring morality back into national politics, and in the activities of her son, who continues to defy cynical political analysts by being the only ex-president in anyone's memory to dedicate his postpresidential years to helping others as a fearless freelance international diplomat, willing to go wherever his assistance can help avoid bloodshed. One hell of a woman and a fierce first-rate-belle to the bitter end, Miz Lillian would be proud of her son, the very spit out of her own consciousness-raising mouth.

66[K]eep fighting for freedom and justice, beloveds, but don't you forget to have fun doin' it. Lord, let your laughter ring forth. Be outrageous, ridicule the fraidy-cats, rejoice in all the oddities that freedom can produce. And when you get through kickin' ass and celebratin' the sheer joy of a good fight, be sure to tell those who come after how much fun it was.**99**

   —*Molly Ivins*

First Lady from Plains

$\mathcal{R}$osalynn Carter was tagged by the national press as a "steel magnolia," so she simply took the label over and gave it a whole new meaning. She was born in 1930 in Plains, Georgia, into the elusively slow and lazy days of rural southern life; but things took an abrupt turn at her father's death when she was thirteen. Plunged almost instantly into helping her mother keep the family afloat by working after school (and still managing to be valedictorian of her high school class), Rosalynn began her journey along the hard road which would come to define much of her life. But for all the challenges thrown in her path, she never backed down and almost always emerged both a little tougher and as gracious as ever.

Ironically, for the woman eventually married to "The Man from Plains," it seems that one of the effects of the tough times she endured was a strong desire to escape Plains—forever. She never quite made it. Her early efforts were modest at best, moving on to a junior college just down the road in Americus; and, if leaving Plains behind was the ultimate goal, she made a fatal move in wrangling herself an introduction to best friend Ruth Carter's brother, Jimmy. At the time it must have sounded promising though, he being an up-and-coming cadet at the U.S. Naval Academy. Indeed, for a few years after marrying the son of a peanut farmer, they moved in circles well outside of Plains: getting as far as Pearl Harbor in Hawaii, before Jimmy's father died, she was brought back—accepting, but saddened—to care for the family farm.

Back in Georgia, Jimmy began to dabble in local politics. Thrown into the role of farmer/politician's wife, Rosalynn learned accounting, campaigning, and the fine art of being a public figure—the latter being by far the most difficult of the bunch. Her style— quiet graciousness balanced with determination and strength—was suited to her southern roots and reinforced by close association with her mother-in-law, the already legendary Miz Lillian. By the time Jimmy entered the Georgia statehouse, Rosalynn was a polished politician with her own agenda—principally the support and advocacy for mentally and emotionally handicapped children, which she was not in the least bit shy about pursuing.

During Jimmy's three-year-long run for the presidency, Rosalynn proved herself one of the all time best road warriors, crisscrossing the nation countless times, rallying to whip up the troops time and again. When the Carters finally strolled down Pennsylvania Avenue and into the White House, Rosalynn had once fought her way out of Plains again. She threw herself into the national policy scene with a seriousness and determination unseen in first ladies since Eleanor Roosevelt. Rosalynn acted very much as her husband's partner, attending cabinet meetings and important briefings, and maintaining a running weekly work session with her husband.

In a way, Rosalynn planted the seed that Hillary Clinton would later reap both positively and negatively. She carved out a powerful role for first ladies; but she also attracted the attention of those who tend to froth at the mouth at the thought of women in power. And, if the beltway establishment was unprepared for the introspective deep morality of Jimmy Carter, it was totally unprepared for a woman who had no fear of operating with grace and strength in the midst of so much power. That unpreparedness, combined with her southern charm (Rosalynn, unlike Hillary, would never, for example, have responded to criticism of her hands-on role by sarcastically suggesting that maybe she stay home and bake cookies), kept the "anti-powerful first ladies" lobby at bay for much of her tenure in Washington—at least until she became a very enthusiastic and very public supporter of the Equal Rights Amendment.

When Jimmy Carter's presidency was brought down after only one short term by a bad turn of the economy and a Hollywood actor riding a Republican agenda, Rosalynn and he returned to Plains, crushed and defeated. But after a period of mourning, she re-emerged with an autobiography, *First Lady from Plains*, that received glowing reviews; and once again actively pursues her own belle-ish agenda along with her husband (just now gaining the political respect he had been previously denied). They have subsequently devoted much of their lives to Habitat for Humanity, a nationwide organization that builds low-cost housing for the poor.

HOGG HEARTED

A Texas legend, as much for the stories and snickers caused by her name as for her life as the most philanthropic Lone Star doyenne of her time, **Ima Hogg** was born in 1882, in the dusty town of Mineola. She grew up in the stormy (and often convoluted) eye of Texas politics (her father was a big time reform governor in the last years of the 19th century); and died ninety-three years later on a mission to hear "the world's best music" one last time at the London Symphony. Contrary to modern lore, Ima did not have a sister named "Ura" nor was the odd name an attempt by her father to instill humility — Ima was the name of the heroine in an poem written by Big Daddy Hogg's brother. A colorful name from the annals of history, Ima Hogg is now the contemporary tag for a legion of budding Texas drag queens.

The Lady President

Of all the southern women that traveled in political circles, **Edith Bolling Wilson** typified the fantasy of how a proper southern lady should act. A renowned hostess and party giver, charming, sexy enough to make the Washington press scandalized at the president's attentions, but not sensational enough to prove a political liability, she was devilishly witty, yet balanced by impeccable manners. She was also strong enough to protect her husband in his time of deepest need and to act as "Steward" of the United States (some say taking over the reins completely), while her husband recuperated from a near-fatal stroke.

Edith, born into an old Virginia family, completed her formal education at a "finishing" school in Arlington. At twenty-four, she married Norman Galt, a Washington jeweler, with whom she had a son who died shortly after birth. Five years later, Norman died, and Edith— still stunningly beautiful—settled quietly into the life of a well-to-do widow. By happenstance, she became acquainted with Woodrow Wilson's cousin and, as a result, the president himself. Within the year, after a romance that both horrified and titillated the entire Washington social scene (he'd only been widowed for seven months), the president convinced her to marry him, and thus she became the First Lady on December 18, 1915.

Edith Wilson was the model wife and constant companion of her husband. He shared dispatches with her, taught her his secret code, and discussed all the issues of state with her, often referring to her as his most trusted advisor. He was in love; and she was the source of his strength and optimism.

On October 2, 1919, Woodrow Wilson suffered a massive stoke that completely incapacitated him. Told by the president's physician that to resign would kill him, but knowing he needed complete and totally uninterrupted rest, Edith did what any good wife would: she took over her husband's responsibilities until he was strong enough to resume his position. Because the media was not what it is today, the true extent of Wilson's serious condition was kept from everyone but a handful of White House insiders. Similarly, the true extent to which Edith actually ran the country will probably never be known since the only people who saw the president in those stressful months were the Wilsons' private physicians. Despite more than one visit by a delegation of Senate and Cabinet members, strong-willed Edith was adamant that no one would be allowed to see her husband.

To the delegations, Edith would dutifully report that the only decisions she made were the judgments about what was important enough to disturb her husband's recuperation. Then she would dutifully turn over the requested documents to the inquiring Cabinet member with a scribbled note that began, "The president instructs . . ." Apparently no one was willing to cross or question her; and so she pulled it off, sticking to her story till her death—even though more than one legislator grumbled that Woodrow Wilson's signature had begun to bear a striking resemblance to Edith's.

She drew the line, however, when Wilson, after a partial recovery, suggested running for office again in 1920. Adamant belle Edith, having held off the hounds of Congress by adjunctively and judiciously running the country for one year, declared that enough was simply enough and put her foot down.

Empress Hillary

*T*one-deaf Grammy-award winner, unproven baker of cookies, and unfortunate heir to the legacy of first ladies-with-brains, **Hillary Rodham Clinton,** one of Arkansas' best and brightest was a walking target by the time she hit Washington. In a smiling reprisal of the old slogan "Two Governors for the Price of One," Bill Clinton offered the "Buy One, Get One Free" deal. The only problem was what went down okay in Texas (after all, Ma Ferguson was supposed to be a figurehead for Pa) did not go down well in Presidential Land, particularly when it turned out that "Empress Hillary" proved smarter than her elected husband.

If the truth be told, Hillary could do no right. Crucified for trying to actually bring meaningful healthcare reform to the nation, blasted for appearing too vampish in a fashion layout in *Vogue*, accused of being the criminal mastermind behind a Whitewater scandal that no one has ever been able to figure out (it was the real Hillary-haters who wanted to prove how damned nefarious they believe she is), she was blasted by her so-called supporters for doing such a bang-up job of avoiding the spotlight so husband Bill could get re-elected.

Though born and raised in Chicago, Hillary, by virtue of environment, marriage, and default, has become the defacto renegade belle of the Arkansas smart set. In a country where people are obsessed with her hairstyles (mostly the officially sanctioned and typical southern frosted, helmet head) and intimidated by a Wellesley-educated belle-with-a-brain, someday we may even get the chance to elect a president (and perhaps a "true" daughter of the South) as smart as Hillary. In the meantime, we hope she continues to raise our consciousness (and a little hell) and keep them guessing all the way.

A Token

The first woman sworn in as a United States Senator may sound like a monumental occasion, but it came about as a result of a largely cynical plot. In September 1922, Georgia Senator Thomas Watson died in office. One month later, **Rebecca Latimer Felton** was appointed to serve in the vacant position until a new election could be held—Congress not being in session at the time. Rebecca, an eighty-seven-year-old suffragette and pawn, was appointed by then-Governor Thomas Hardwick to deflect attention away from the fact that he had lead the fight that resulted in his state being one of the few to reject the 19th Amendment giving women the right to vote.

Women's suffrage had won ratification just two short years prior and, like it or not, the Georgia politicos were going to have to deal with women voters. And so the governor decided to give the people a worn-out figurehead for a week as a slap in the face.

But sop or symbol, Rebecca took her job as far as she could, pressuring Walter George, the man elected in the special election, into delaying presenting his credentials until she could be swore in. She had to endure a long-winded speech from one of the western senators detailing all the reasons why women were unsuited for such business, but she was eventually sworn in. In her one and only speech, she scolded the collected body by telling them "you will get ability" when women join your ranks.

In her long career of activism, Rebecca Felton was not only a leader of the Georgian suffrage movement but had fought a three-decade-long battle against the convict leasing system then entrenched in Georgia. Seen by Rebecca as little more than a new form of slavery, convict leasing was the rental of prisoners by the state government to local businesses who paid no wages to the workers, only a fee to the state. Her efforts against the practice did little to win her friends among the local farmers exploiting the low cost labor; and it wasn't until 1908 that she finally succeeded in getting it abolished.

❝ I like bravery . . . If you can't do it, find out why you can't do it. Don't just say, 'Well they are going to do what they want to do anyway, stay home' . . . It has done a lot of harm to us. ❞

— *Christina Daniels Adair, Texas suffragette and civil rights leader, born 1893*

ADOPTED BELLE

*D*olley Madison was called the Lady Presidentress during her eight year co-habitation at the White House with husband James (after all, the democracy was still young and various things were unclear). But it was during her tenure that the press started calling her First Lady, the appropriate appellation still used today. Indeed, since both Washington's and Adams' terms ended before the White House was completed, Dolley had first dibs on setting a great deal of social precedent and protocol. She'd been given a head start at it, having served as the unofficial hostess for widower Thomas Jefferson.

Born into a good Pennsylvania Quaker family, Dolley (like Hillary years later) became a Southerner by marriage (her second) when she charmed Virginia's famous founding father, James Madison. It seems "turning Southern" (a tradition later adapted by other Washington wives with pretensions toward southern-styled civility) wore well on Dolley who became renowned in her time as a superbly gracious hostess (very important in those early days when the new bumpkin politicians were more than a little queasy about embarrassing themselves in front of visiting European dignitaries). But if Dolley managed to charm the pants off of everyone within hailing distance of Washington (James Madison's twice-defeated rival, Charles Pinckney, once lamented that he would have had a fair chance had it not been for Dolley!), she never compromised her zest for life in the process. Though not belle-born, but belle-well-learned, Dolley was regularly spotted publicly smoking tobacco, playing cards, and cutting quite a swath across the dance floor.

Dolley did the entire United States population a big favor in 1817. Years before, when Thomas Jefferson was in Europe, he tasted a concoction soon to be known as ice cream, and brought back one of the machines used to make the delicacy. He introduced it to Dolley; and she fell in love with the sweet treat (proving she must have had some southern blood after all). While planning her husband's inaugural party, she included it on the menu. When newspapers nationwide printed the menu, a craze for ice cream swept the country, continuing to this day.

And Dolley beat the fictional Scarlett O'Hara to the heroic punch by some fifty years when she refused to panic and leave the White House during the war of 1812, at a time when most of the Washington citizenry was already high-tailing it out of town. She stayed, despite the frantic urgings of her husband occupied at the front, until the British cannons were booming over the city and the White House was ablaze (causing scorching which can still be seen to this day). Even then, she calmly picked through the White House papers and artifacts, taking important items, and, in a gesture of lasting symbolic value, carried the now-famous portrait of George Washington away to safety, as well as a portrait of herself in decollete.

❝I would rather fight with my hands than my tongue.**❞**
— *Dolley Madison*

THE SILVER ROSE OF TEXAS

$\mathscr{T}$he invasion of southern women into politics was no simple matter. Making the transition from "ladyhood" to political power took years of determined effort. First it took grabbing a toehold, then squeezing out more and more territory to stand on, all the while smiling sweetly over your shoulder in order to calm the boys. It's been a long impressive journey; and it took until 1989 and **Ann Richards,** before the old mold was broken once and for all.

Ann Richards was one of a growing group of women that had taken over control of all but the highest political positions in Texas — mayors of virtually all the big cities, including Dallas, Houston, San Antonio, Austin, Corpus Cristi, and El Paso, county commissioners (Ann made her start as the commissioner of Travis County), and council members scattered all across the state. There have been many theories for this phenomenon, ranging from the quip that Texan men simply decided to let the women do the hard work to the more realistic proposition that the Texas good-ol'-boy network was so intractably corrupt that the only possible way to get an honest politician was to elect a woman.

Whatever the reason, the bullish belles made inroads, but the battles were still fought according to the old school rules. The first big step up the ladder, however, was taken by Ann when she became Treasurer of the State in 1982. Then in 1990, she won big time, battling through one of the ugliest and weirdest campaigns of all time to become the governor of Texas. She entered the race in stellar form. After an eight-year stint as Treasurer, generally credited with doing a fine job, particularly given the mess she was left with, she made a name for herself on the national scene with her bitingly belle-ish, funny keynote address at the 1988 Democratic National Convention, where she delivered the sterling line about George Bush, "Poor George, he just can't help it. He was born with a silver foot in his mouth."

Smart, experienced, attractive, and funny too: this woman had it all, plus almost zero negative ratings all across Texas. But then came the primary against ex-Governor Mark White and then Attorney General and vicious campaigner Jim Mattox. With a wealth of serious issues to contend with in a state that had been mismanaged into the ground, the primary ended up being a contest about who was the most bloodthirsty of them all. Charging up the electric chair and wiping out "all them scumbags" on death row became the battle cry—and that was only the beginning.

Ann had to go through a run-off election against Jim Mattox; and this time the mud-slinging tactics sank below sea level. When Ann, a recovering alcoholic and veteran of the '60s in liberal Austin, where everyone had at least tried marijuana, was asked if she had ever done drugs, she resolutely refused to answer. Gentleman Jim spent the rest of the campaign attempting to paint a picture of Ann Richards wallowing around in the drug underworld, stoned out of her mind. Refusing to answer may have been a tactical mistake on her part. Journalist Molly Ivins suggested Ann's best defense would have been to claim she was too drunk to remember; but Ann stuck to her guns and won a narrow victory.

That got her to the general election; and then the down and dirty became out-and-out bizarre. Her Republican opponent, Clayton Williams, was an absolute throw-back to the days where money meant everything. Filthy rich (oil, cattle, and banking), he never held public office before but wanted to "serve for the good of Texas," and was generally well-liked and way ahead in the polls. Ann seemingly had no chance, unless Clayton screwed up, which he obligingly did—over and over and over again. From telling tasteless rape jokes to the press, to admitting he didn't know what Proposition

One (the only proposition) on the ballot was about, to reminiscing about going to Mexico to "get serviced" when he was in college, Clayton Williams flailed. In the end, Ann Richards won one of the strangest election ordeals in history—because the state of Texas, disgusted at having its dirty political laundry hung out for all the world to see, decided to elect a woman to clean the mess up.

After a high-profile ride in office including a cover shot for *Texas Monthly*, in which an Ann Richards impersonator, geared up in full white leather, sat astride a giant Harley Davidson, the governor fell from power. Perhaps in a vicarious gesture of revenge for her joke at the former president's expense, she was defeated in her bid for re-election by his son, none other than George Bush, Jr.

66 The roosters may crow, but the hens deliver the goods. **99**
   —*Ann Richards*

Hell-Raising Writer

*W*hen it comes to southern women politicos, one of the very best is in a category all by herself, living well out there raising hell. **Molly Ivins** never held office, but she's made more people wet their pants laughing at her incisive and hilarious unpeeling of politics — Texas style — than you can possibly count.

Molly got her start working for pennies on the *Texas Observer* and carved out a style of political reportage that is as bone-rattlingly on target as it is outrageously funny. In 1976, she was hired away by the *New York Times,* a mismatch from the very start. Trying to squeeze Molly's vivid imagery into the tight little columns of the *Times* just wasn't going to work; and she was finally fired for, as she puts it, "describing a community chicken-killing festival as 'a gang pluck.'"

Back to Texas and the *Dallas Times-Herald* where — and here we should all stop and give thanks — she was told she could write whatever she wanted to, however she wanted to. This being Molly Ivins, it didn't take long to test their sincerity. The paper was swamped with letters and complaints after she had questioned a local congressman's intelligence by writing, "If his IQ slips any lower, we'll have to water him twice a day." True to their word, the newspaper came to her defense with a bold billboard campaign that read "Molly Ivins Can't Say That, Can She?" Molly gratefully borrowed that slogan for the title of her first book, which should be required reading for anyone who cares remotely about politics or just loves to simply laugh out loud.

66 It's illegal to be gay in Texas again, thanks to the Fifth Circuit. They reinstated our sodomy statute so people can legally screw pigs in public, but not each other in private. **99**
—*Molly Ivins*

A WANTON WOMAN

𝒞onnie Hamzy is not exactly a politician yet; but she's trying. In 1996, the self-proclaimed rock and roll groupie ran for Congress as an Independent from Arkansas. When that didn't work, she ran for Little Rock City Commissioner. The Little Rock resident is well known in rock circles; she was immortalized by Grand Funk Railroad in their 1973 hit, "We're An American Band." And, in 1992, she appeared nude in *Penthouse* for $50,000, accompanied by an article in which she not only discussed her sex life with rock musicians, but alleged that she also was propositioned by Bill Clinton in 1984 by the swimming pool of a Little Rock hotel. They kissed passionately and groped, claims Connie, but never consummated the relationship.

"There's not a damn thing in the Constitution that says a groupie can't run for Congress," she exclaimed in an interview in the *Arkansas Democrat-Gazette*. Her platform included jobs (pro), abortion (ditto), marijuana legalization (surprise!) and lawyers (anti). Her campaign slogan was "I'm not a lawyer." She lost both electoral bids, but was not without support: "Everyone in my family voted for her," reports a woman from Little Rock, "because she walks a fine line of being wacko and having more sense than anyone else."

Connie likes to go topless, which recently got her into trouble. She was arrested and fined $50 for wearing only a thong bikini bottom in a public park. And it may have lost her some credibility when it came to the Clinton story too. When she approached a reporter from the *Los Angeles Times* in 1992 to tell her tale, she handed him a topless photo of herself.

She's written an autobiography, which so far has not been published. And there's no word on whether she intends to continue pursuing public office.

❝ I may be a slut, but I'm no liar. **❞**   —*Connie Hamzy*

Presidential Paramours?

Bill Clinton likes women, particularly Southern women. Or so the rumors go, anyway. Here's a list of the belles who have allegedly kept him company:

- Arkansan **Susan McDougal.** Reputedly they were lovers during the Whitewater heyday, which is why she is refusing to testify against him. Vehemently denied by both parties; Susan claims the rumor demonstrates just how low the press will go.

- **Gennifer Flowers Shelnut,** ex-cabaret singer who supposedly had a twelve-year liaison with the saxophone-playing politician and has subsequently made big bucks selling her story and posing nude for *Penthouse*. (She got $200,000 from the magazine.)

- Former Miss Arkansas, **Sally Perdue,** who boasts of a four-month affair in Little Rock; she would sing "He's Just My Bill"; he called her "Long Tall Sally." Also made money subsequently posing for *Penthouse* ($50,000).

- **Lencola Sullivan,** another former Miss Arkansas, who also was reportedly the former girlfriend of blind singer and musician Stevie Wonder.

- Former Miss America **Elizabeth Ward** allegedly had an affair with Clinton in Little Rock in 1982. She neither confirms nor denies the rumor, but posed for *Playboy* for $100,000 in an unrelated story.

- **Bobbie Ann Williams,** who not only claims she had sex multiple times with the prez in Little Rock while a prostitute, but also supposedly has a child by him "who is the spittin' image" of old Bill. Made $25,000 telling the story to a tabloid.

- **Deborah Mathis,** a former reporter for the *Arkansas Gazette*, who has sold no stories or photos of herself—yet.

5

Sweet Southern Songbirds

Whether it's blues, gospel, or country, the South's got a major hold on authentic American music. And, as you will see in these pages, some mighty fine women turned out to have been at the forefront of each one of these genres. These women found fame and fortune on their own terms; but somehow changing their names didn't seem to hurt nothin' either.

THE SALT OF THE EARTH AND SASSY TO BOOT

There is just something about **Patsy Cline** that the American imagination won't let go of. Perhaps it was her death in a tragic plane crash at the age of thirty. Or maybe it was her unbridled sexuality, consummate confidence, and foul mouth during a time — the buttoned down '50s — when women weren't supposed to say such things; but boisterous belle Patsy did anyway. "She had a mouth like a sailor, and she didn't put on airs. She was just Patsy, comfortable in her skin. I admired that." remembers Vivian

Liberto — first wife of singer Johnny "The Man in Black" Cash, in a recent profile of Patsy for the *New York Times Magazine*. "But that beautiful voice and body were so different from her . . . roughness."

Most likely, though, her continued fame comes from her voice — full-bodied and oozing raw emotion and feeling. "When she sang a ballad —" remembered friend and fellow Grand Ole Opry performer Dottie West, "you know, a real tearjerker — and you'd see her crying, Patsy wasn't faking . . . No one could sing the blues like Patsy. Her troubles may have added to her greatness as a singer."

Trouble did seem to dog the Winchester, Virginia, country girl. Born Virginia Patterson Hensley in 1932, her first idol was Shirley

Temple; but her peripatetic family could not afford the singing or dancing lessons she begged for. By the time she was ten, she was determined to become a country music singer, despite a difficult home life—her parents were constantly breaking up; and Patsy once hinted at sexual abuse by her father. A bout with rheumatic fever at age thirteen left her with a "booming voice like Kate Smith," said Pasty in a 1957 interview. When times got tough for her family, the feisty fourteen year old, passing for sixteen, went to work at a poultry factory, plucking chickens, later working at a drugstore. "Experience is a hard teacher," she once noted, "She gives the tests first."

But she was more determined than ever to make it, spending every available hour singing at parties, church socials, and the like, protecting herself from men who got too close. "Nothing men do surprise me," she once said. "I'm ready for them. I know how to whack below the belt." Apparently she could always take care of herself. Dottie West recalls that when she knew her, "It was common knowledge you didn't mess with 'the Cline'. If you kicked her, she kicked right back." She did take help when offered, though. In 1952, she met Bill Peer, who gave her the first stage name she used, Patsy Hensley, got her the first gigs of her career, and fell head over heels in love with her. Patsy didn't reciprocate his affections completely. In the middle of their torrid love affair, she married Gerald Cline, juggling the two of them (plus a few other beaus), as well as a burgeoning career in Nashville. She got her big break in 1957, winning the Arthur Godfrey Talent Scout contest at the age of twenty-four, performing the classic, "Walkin' After Midnight." Over the next six years, she became the first country western female singer ever to crossover successfully on both country and popular music charts. She also divorced Gerald, married Charlie Dick in another tempestuous pairing, and had two children.

And she was fearless! Once, recalled singer Roger Miller, a bunch of musicians had gone to Mexico to buy grass and were concerned about getting back over the Texas border. Patsy stuffed it down her bra, saying, "What the hell y'all worried about when you got the Cline here?" At the height of her fame, she was in a car accident that tore up her face and nearly killed her, a near miss only to be followed two years later by the fatal plane crash that did take her life, and the lives of three other Opry stars. Her epitaph rings true with the haunting and prophetic, "Death cannot kill what never dies."

A star for only five years, the amazing Patsy Cline's enormous talent lives on. In 1973, she posthumously became the first solo woman artist to be inducted into the Country Music Hall of Fame. A 1985 movie of her life story, *Sweet Dreams*, starring Jessica Lange, brought her music to a whole new generation. Over thirty years after her death, her albums continue to be among the top sellers for MCA and there continue to be revivals, including all-Patsy nights at the Ryman Auditorium in Nashville where her classics "Crazy," "Blue Moon of Kentucky," and many more, pushed her down the road to infamy.

66Here's to those who wish us well and those who don't can go to hell!**99**
 —*Patsy Cline*

"Jest A Semple" Country Gal

The legendary **Dolly** "I pattern my look after Cinderella, Mother Goose, and the local hooker" **Parton** sure knows how to poke fun at herself. When asked about her often over the top wigs she joyfully says, "Lots of women buy just as many wigs and make-up and things as I do . . . they just don't wear them all at the same time." Commenting on her famously ample bosom, she once declared, "I do have big tits. Always had 'em. Pushed 'em up, whacked 'em around. Why not make fun of 'em? I made a fortune with 'em." And on her long marriage to little seen Carl Dean, she has this to say, "We met at the Wishy Washy and its been wishy washy ever since."

But there's nothing wishy washy about Dolly. Hers is a true rags to riches tale, in which a platinum blonde heroine escapes the poverty of the foothills of the Great Smoky Mountains and finds fame and fortune living happily ever after, never forgetting her humble roots. She was born in 1946 in Locust Ridge, Tennessee, so poor her share-cropper daddy couldn't afford to pay the doctor's fee for her birth, "so he gave him a sack of cornmeal. I have often joked that I have been raking in the dough ever since." The lack of money never interfered with young Dolly's quest for glamour—in her dime-store days, she would rouge her lips with mercurochrome.

One of twelve children—"we liked to tease Momma, say she always had one on her and one in her"—Dolly debuted at the Grand Ole Opry at thirteen. When she graduated high school (the first in her family), she hightailed it off to Nashville where she was given her first big break by Porter Waggoner, who offered her $60,000 a year to sing and hawk dishtowels ("you can't buy 'em, you can only get 'em . . . in boxes of Breeze") and menstrual tonics on his television show. "I appeared on TV long before my family owned one," quipped Dolly. The two singers, who won awards for Vocal Duo of the

Year in 1968, 1970, and 1971, eventually parted ways in a purported none-too-friendly manner. She wanted her own show; he wanted her to stay with him. But the collaboration was smooth in the beginning and with her first paychecks, she bought a Cadillac and redecorated her parents' home.

Launching out on her own in the early '70s, the diminutive singer-songwriter soon became the best known country music singer in the world. Her first number one record was "Joshua" in 1970; and the next year saw "Old Time Preacher Man" win a BMI songwriting award. She has recorded over seventy albums and 300 of her own songs. Her hits include: "Jolene," "My Coat of Many Colors," and "I Will Always Love You," her farewell to Porter (a song re-recorded by Whitney Houston for the soundtrack of the movie, *The Bodyguard*, that became a monster hit, again assuring Dolly of many more bucks from royalties as its songwriter). She did get her own television show—briefly, twice in fact—and was named Country

Music Female Vocalist of the Year in 1975 and 1976. In 1977, she recorded the number one pop and country duet "Islands In the Stream" with Kenny Rogers and won a Grammy for Best Country Female Performance in 1978, for "Here You Come Again," and in 1981, for "9 to 5."

The '80s saw her take off on the big screen when she starred in the movies *9 to 5*, *The Best Little Whorehouse in Texas*, and *Steel Magnolias*. At that time, she became instant tabloid fodder; once, she claimed, she tried a "Dolly Parton Diet" that one was touting—but didn't lose any weight. In May, 1986, she opened Dollywood, a personalized theme park featuring her trademark butterfly in Pigeon Forge, Tennessee. It contains a

---

NASHVILLE'S NEWEST HIT GIRL

Did I Shave My Legs for This? is the debut album of hot-as-a-southern-summer-evening **Deana Carter,** who was recently predicted by *The New York Times Magazine* to succeed Dolly Parton and Shania Twain as country music's next sex symbol. The thirty-one-year-old blonde, who six years ago worked as a janitor cleaning urinals, when told of the *Times'* mention, exclaimed, "All I can do is look down at my breasts and go, 'Wow Dolly and Shania have got me beat!'" Her song tells the woman's side of typical country fare—the end of a relationship with a drunk live-in lover. The Goodlettsville, Tennessee, native, who was named for Dean Martin, recently found wedded bliss with fellow Nashville musician, Chris DeCroice. Reports *People* about her marriage, "She'll keep shaving her legs for him."

replica of her childhood home and a museum depicting her life story. Always socially responsible and involved in the community, in 1992, she donated $500,000 to help improve public education in her native home of Sevier County, Tennessee.

Despite her recording "Dumb Blonde" in 1967, she is "not offended by all the dumb blonde jokes. Because I know I'm not dumb. And I also know I'm not blonde." She makes no bones about living apart from her husband most of the time: "People ask me if I believe in living together before marriage . . . I don't believe in living together after marriage." In her autobiography, she discusses her close friendship with childhood friend Judy Ogle, with whom she travels, sleeps in the same bed, and owns an apartment in New York City (along with longtime pal, male music producer Sandy Gallin). But, insists Dolly, she and Judy are not lovers. Recently reported to be working on a dance-mix and video version of the former Cat Stevens hit "Peace Train" with Madonna's brother Christopher Ciccone, Dolly's superstardom knows no limits. A firebrand from the word go, somehow she pulls it all off happily, always with a big smile on her face. As Burt Reynolds once said "How could you not like Dolly Parton? That woman is human sunshine."

66I've been accused of everything and I'm guilty of most of it.**99**
    —*Dolly Parton*

"THE STRADIVARIUS OF SINGERS"

The great diva **Leontyne Price,** who was the first black woman to achieve world-wide status as *prima donna assoluta,* was born and raised in Laurel, Mississippi. A child of the Depression, Mary Violet Leontyne grew up singing in the church choir and playing the piano. When she was nine, she heard Marion Anderson sing, which provided her with a wake up call. "I was thrilled with this woman's manner, her carriage, her pride, her voice," she later told *Ebony.* It wasn't until Leotyne was in college on a scholarship, however, when a teacher encouraged her to explore the full range of her voice (she had been singing alto), that her vocal abilities began to be noticed. Switching to Julliard, she first attended an opera and became determined to become an opera singer, despite the limited roles for African Americans and her own lack of knowledge of foreign languages.

With hard work, an iron will to succeed, and a great deal of charm and beauty, as well as a fabulous voice, she did it. The young soprano made her stage debut in 1951 and the next year appeared as the female lead in an enormously successful revival of *Porgy and Bess.* Her "acting is as fiery as her singing," reported the *Washington Post* at the time. Later, she did a grand tour of Europe, singing *Aida,* and became the first black person to appear in opera on television. She seemed to gain as much attention for her regal stature and grace as her voice. Raved the *New York Times,* in describing her Aida, "She was Aida of such physical attractiveness that, for once, it was thoroughly understandable that Radames should prefer her to the highborn princess." She herself credited her success to a voice that she called "dark" and "smoky" and to the "luxury of my Blackness."

In 1961, she made her Metropolitan Opera debut where she received an unprecedented forty-five-minute standing ovation. She once stated, "For a long time the only

time I felt beautiful—in the sense of being complete as a woman, as a human being, and even female—was when I was singing." In the '60s, she gave 118 performances at the Metropolitan, but reduced her appearances during the '70s because "I [was] beginning to forget what I started out with—the completely natural joy of singing. It's almost coming back, and I'm trying not to lose it." Between the late '70s and 1985, when she retired, Leontyne concentrated mostly on recitals, singing and recording spirituals, Christmas carols, hymns, and songs by contemporary composers.

Among the many awards bestowed upon this twelve-time Grammy winner are the Presidential Medal of Freedom; and she has also been honored as an American Academy of Arts and Sciences' Fellow. While she lives in New York City, she visits her hometown of Laurel often and gave one of the first ever nonsegregated recitals there. Not one to hide her accomplishments under a bushel, she is particularly proud of her trailblazing: "To the end of time," she told *Opera News*, "I will be the vehicle for major exposure for young black artists—sopranos, baritones, the whole thing."

❝I totally and completely admit, with no qualms at all, my egomania, my selfishness, coupled with a really magnificent voice.**❞**

      —Leontyne Price

THE BLACK SWAN

Elizabeth Greenfield Taylor (1819-1876) was the first African American musician to earn fame in both Europe and the United States. Born a slave in Natchez, Mississippi, she was freed in childhood by her owner, whose neighbor gave Elizabeth musical lessons. Blessed with a voice that had a range of over three octaves, she was dubbed the "The Black Swan" and once gave a command performance before Queen Victoria. Befriended by Harriet Beecher Stowe, who also promoted her, she was compared most to Jenny Lind and often called an "African Nightingale."

The Belle Of Butcher "Holler"

*T*he legendary image of the tough-yet-tender working class southern woman pulling herself up by the bootstraps is almost as popular as that of Scarlett O'Hara; and country singer **Loretta Lynn's** colorful life story is largely responsible for its mythological origins. Loretta was born in 1937 in Butcher "Holler," Kentucky, the second of eight children to "a poor but proud mountain family" notes *Definitive Country*. One of her sisters is Crystal Gayle (originally Brenda Gail Webb and self-renamed for Krystal Hamburgers), also a country singer. At age thirteen, Loretta married Oliver "Mooney"— so named because of his moonshine days in Kentucky—Lynn, a.k.a. "Doo" for Doo-little which is what Loretta likes to call him because he does, in fact, do so little. Loretta began to have children at age fourteen, maintaining in her autobiography that she "never knew where babies came from until it happened to me." By twenty-eight, this mother of six was also a grandmother.

She sang only for her family until she was twenty-three and reached success with the release of her very first album, *I'm a Honky Tonk Girl,* which she also wrote. Having no money for promotion, she and her husband mailed out copies of the record with a letter asking disk jockeys to play it. Traveling from juke joint to juke joint she backed up the album with live appearances. When the record hit big, the couple were off to Nashville and a waiting recording contract.

Loretta premiered at the Grand Ole Opry in 1960, but didn't have the de rigeur nice dress and high heels—again no money—and so was looked upon as a country bumpkin in boots and an old dress by the other women appearing that night. Soon after, however, she was a star singing "if you're lookin' at me, you're lookin' at country" and could afford any dress she wanted. Named Country Music Association (CMA) Female Vocalist of the Year in 1967 and again in 1972 and 1973, in 1972, she was the first woman to ever be named CMA's Entertainer of the Year. Often a collaborator with good friend Conway Twitty, they shared the CMA Vocal Duo Award from 1972-1975. She was the very first guest star on the seminal country music television show *Hee Haw*, when it premiered on June 15, 1969, on CBS.

She has released over fifty albums, many of which are filled with her own compositions. Her beloved songs include "Success," "The Pill," (which is credited with liberalizing country music attitudes and of which Loretta jokes, "they didn't have none of them pills when I was younger, or I'd have been swallowing 'em like popcorn"), "Rated X," and "Out of My Head and Into My Bed."

She claims in her autobiography that her marriage hasn't always been easy. Her husband kicked her out when she was two months pregnant for the first time; she was extremely sexually inexperienced (she *was* only fourteen) and even the dog wouldn't eat her cooking, claimed Doo. But they reconciled; and she learned to defend her turf. She even wrote a song about it, "Fist City," in which a woman was making a play for Doo and "I let her know she was gonna get a mouthful of knuckles if she kept it up. And I'd have done it. I've always had a bad temper when it came to seeing women make eyes at my man."

She is now semi-retired and enjoying life at

her home, Hurricane Hills. The movie about her life, *Coal Miner's Daughter*, based on her autobiography of the same name, garnered Sissy Spacek an Academy Award in 1980 and is often credited with bringing renewed fame and interest to Patsy Cline. Patsy and Loretta were very good friends; and Patsy is featured prominently in both the movie and book, which created an explosion of interest in the deceased singer. In what is perhaps an ultimate among true southern honors, a twelve-mile section of Tennessee Highway 13 was renamed in Loretta's honor in June, 1994.

THE TEXAS TORNADO

Texas wild-child singer **Tanya Tucker** cut her teeth and first record at age nine and blasted to fame in 1972 at the age of fourteen, appearing provocatively on the cover of *Rolling Stone* magazine. Her hits include, "Delta Dawn," "Blood Red and Goin' Down," and "What's Your Mama's Name?" A kind-hearted hell-raiser, she is reputed to have broken up Glenn Campbell's marriage and is now the single mother of two children. When chosen to sing the National Anthem at the 1992 GOP Convention, she took the opportunity to blast then Vice-President Quayle for his dimwitted crack about television's *Murphy Brown* promoting single motherhood: "What in the world does he know what it's like to go through pregnancy?" Dan did not respond. Tanya is still very active on the country music scene and has recently told her life story in *Nickel Dreams*.

The Tejano Music Queen

$\mathcal{B}$orn in 1971, **Selena Quintanilla-Perez,** the Hispanic superstar singer known simply as Selena, began singing in a house band at the age of seven with her brother on bass, and sister on drums, in her family's restaurant in Corpus Christi, Texas. She sang professionally by the age of nine, at which time her family hit the road in pursuit of a musical career. Of Mexican-American descent, the young singer did not speak Spanish as a child, but learned quickly once she started singing, hastening her rapid ascent in the male-dominated world of Tejano music (a hybrid of traditional latin, disco, funk, and polka rhythms specific to south Texas and the Mexican border region). Thanks in large part to Selena's phenomenal success, the popularity of Tejano music has skyrocketed from backyard weddings and county fairs to jam-packed arenas and 60,000-seat stadiums.

A strong-willed and beautiful young woman, Selena knew what she wanted early on and had an amazing gift of easy connection with her fans. She began recording some twenty albums and compact discs in 1978, including her multi-gold, 1994 Grammy winner, *Selena Live,* and the phenomenal quadruple platinum, *Amor Prohibido* (Forbidden Love), which debuted at Billboard's number one spot. A millionaire by nineteen, Selena was sought out for several product endorsements including Coca-Cola, Agree Shampoo, and Southwestern Bell. Hailed as the Tex/Mex Madonna, her meteoric rise provided thousands of young Latina women with a role model very much like themselves, and fueled media interest in the Tejano culture and the economic power of the Hispanic consumer. Given to flashy costumes and a deep love of fashion (reflected in her self-named Selena, Etc. boutiques), Selena had a great sense of showmanship; she never forgot to have fun and her videos of disco remakes and love songs convey that passion. She brought financial security to her family, who were heavily involved in her career, and

eventually paved the way for her future husband, Chris Perez (a hard rock guitarist and band member) to become a part of the family. Her talent knew no limits and she toured extensively throughout the United States and Mexico to enormous acclaim and adulation.

But her life came to an abrupt end at the age of twenty-three, when she was shot in the back by Yolanda Saldivar, the former president of her fan club, on March 31, 1995. In a nine-and-one-half-hour standoff with the police, Saldivar hid in a pickup truck threatening suicide, until finally surrendering. She was convicted of murder, and is currently serving a life sentence in prison. In death, the Tejano queen's fame has become astronomical, bringing her nationwide household recognition with the posthumous release of her music (including the smash English language hit "Dreaming of You"), several books, and a movie about her life.

The singer also lives on through the Selena Foundation, created to raise funds for charitable purposes through the use of her name, and Q Productions, a family-owned company dedicated to promoting and developing Tejano artists and music. The Selena Foundation promotes educational causes and funds scholarships throughout Texas, provides assistance for people in crisis, funds drug-awareness programs, and grants money to charities working with disadvantaged and mentally retarded children. In 1995, the late singer was presented the Barbara Jordan Humanitarian Award by the United

Cerebral Palsy of Greater Houston for her charity work. During the same year, the Corpus Christi Municipal Auditorium was renamed in her honor. Recently, on the second anniversary of Selena's death, a fan left flowers on the singer's gravesite with a note reading "To our Queen that will never be forgotten," alluding to her powerful musical legacy and the emotional impact that she had on so many people.

SEEING EYE TO EYE

Atlanta local **Lisa "Left-Eye" Lopes** is one of a trio of singers in the rap/hip-hop/R&B group TLC. The strange moniker comes from her habit of wearing a condom over her left eye during concerts (the group often sings about safe sex). The most successful girl group ever, TLC vaulted to platinumhood with the sales of its second album *Craxysexycool* and number one single "Waterfalls." Left-Eye, T-Boz, and Chillie (the other two thirds of the group) didn't get to cash in on their success, though. As a new group, TLC's contract was not generous; according to the *Los Angeles Times*, of the $92 million their album generated for Arista Records, they were lucky to see a scant $1.2 million. And then there was the little matter of the $527,000 hell-raising homegirl Lisa owed Lloyd's of London for burning down the house of her erstwhile boyfriend, former Falcons football player Andre Rison. So it was Chapter 11 for the Grammy-winning trio in 1995.

STAND BY YOUR MAN? ... WHY?

"*The* First Lady" (dubbed so because she was the first woman country singer to have a million-selling album) was born Virginia Wynette Pugh in 1942 on a dirt farm straddling the Alabama-Mississippi border. The future **Tammy Wynette** likes to say, "My top half was born in Alabama, bottom half in Mississippi. If you don't like it, just turn me around." She was raised by her grandparents; and, by the time she was eight, was working in the cotton fields and dreaming of becoming a big star singing with her idol, George Jones. But at seventeen, she married for the first time (she has had five husbands in all), moved to Tupelo, Mississippi, and became a hairdresser. Within three years, she'd had two children, was pregnant with a third, and her marriage was over.

In need of money, she began appearing on the regional *Country Boy Eddie Show* in Birmingham, Alabama, where she became the only other star besides Elvis to be shown on television from the waist up, because showing a pregnant belly was absolutely verboten in 1965. Two years later, she had her first solo number one hit "I Don't Wanna Play House" and her career was off and running. In 1968 she had four number one hits in a row, including the famous "D-I-V-O-R-C-E" and the Grammy-winning "Stand By Your Man" (which was the largest-selling single in country music for fifteen years), and was named the Country Music Association's Female Vocalist of the Year, as she was again in 1969 and 1970. Tammy wrote "Stand By Your Man" in a twenty-minute recording break, and said the song "is just another way of saying 'I love you'—without reservations." Her success was huge and fast; her 1969 greatest hits album stayed on the charts for a phenomenal sixty weeks.

In 1969, Tammy's childhood dream came true, when she not only met and sang with George Jones, the King of Country Music, but married him in a storybook romance.

Together they charted thirteen duet singles between 1971 and 1980, and rode in the Macy's Thanksgiving Day parade in 1971; but privately their relationship was very stormy. Tammy reportedly endured both physical and emotional abuse from George, who was a notoriously hard-drinking man: "A man can be a drunk sometimes. But a drunk can't be a man," said Tammy after their marriage collapsed in 1975. "I always say

that he (Jones) nipped and I nagged. I guess we were both very good at it." Tammy supposedly once took the car keys away from Jones in an attempt to try and keep him dry; but the crafty country crooner with an unquenchable thirst, rode a riding lawnmower — ten miles — to the closest bar! Rumor has it that to tell George it was over, she rented a flat-bed truck and sang "Your Cheatin' Heart" to him in front of the Grand Ole Opry.

In 1979, she wrote her autobiography, *Stand By Your Man*, which was made into a television movie starring Annette O'Toole. The '80s and '90s were more up and down for the woman who calls herself "the loudest singer in the world." Hits came fewer, although she and belle sisters, Dolly Parton and Loretta Lynn, scored big with *Honky Tonk Angels* in 1993. In 1985, she and fifth husband and manager George Richey had to declare bankruptcy after the collapse of a bank that was financing shopping center investments of theirs. And sadly, Tammy's notoriously bad health (second only to Elizabeth Taylor's) has seen her endure seventeen operations, reportedly causing her to become hooked on painkillers for which she entered the Betty Ford Center for treatment.

She continues to record and tour in a $250,000 Silver Eagle bus with her Pomeranian pal, Killer. Most recently, she has been reincarnated as a disco diva with the musical group the KLF on their dance club hit "Justified and Ancient." In 1997, she sued the *National Enquirer* and the *Star* for what she maintains are false reports of her ill health. An amazing southern girl with soul, spunk, and a heart (and voice) of gold — keep on pushin', sister, we're rootin' for ya'.

❝The sad part about happy endings is that there's nothing to write about.**❞**
— *Tammy Wynette*

WILD WOMEN DO SING THE BLUES

*B*orn in the slave plantations and bred in minstrel tents, the blues are uniquely Southern. Wildly popular after World War I, the blues was a female-dominated musical form in which women sang, in often cynically submissive tones, about the balance of power in relationships: sexual domination, the love of no good men, submission to violence, and fantasies of being violent themselves. A counterpoint to the image of the asexual, emotionally repressed white women of the time, blues singers let it all hang out.

In 1900, fourteen-year-old Gertrude Pridgett was appearing with her parents in a Georgia talent show when she met Will "Pa" Rainey and ran off to join his minstrel show; and thus **"Ma" Rainey** was born. Touring the back roads of Georgia, Alabama, Tennessee, and Virginia, Ma soon hit upon a distinctive style of singing, which she called the blues; and Ma and Pa eventually set up their own troupe. But Pa, it turns out, was just a way-station for Ma, who was arrested in 1925 for "holding a lesbian orgy in her home," according to *The American Women's Almanac*, that netted her "an outlaw image that made her a cultural hero." Ma was quite proud of her gender-bending ways. "Prove it On Me Blues," in which she sings, "They say I do it, ain't nobody caught me," was advertised with a picture of a woman in mannish clothes talking to two ultra-feminine flappers. In the 1920s, when the blues craze was sweeping the nation, Ma recorded over one hundred blues songs, over half of which were original, earning her the title "Queen Mother of the Blues." A white singer with her talent would have made more money; but Ma did live well, buying a house in Georgia, dressing in diamonds, and sporting a $13,000 bus with its own electric generator to light her shows. When she died at age fifty-three, however, her death certificate, strangely enough, listed her occupation as housekeeping.

If Ma was the Queen Mother, then magnificent-voiced **Bessie Smith** was the Empress. Rumor has it that Ma kidnaped Bessie and taught her to sing (not true); but the two were close friends and may have been lovers. Born in Chattanooga in 1894, one of nine children who were orphaned before they reached their teens, Bessie spent her early years singing on street corners and later performed in minstrel shows until she was discovered by record producers (initially she was turned down by several because her voice was "too rough"). She knew how to reach out to the audience with a powerful voice that needed no amplification. Guitarist Danny Barker remembers, "You didn't turn your head when she went on . . . [there was] a similarity between what she was doing and what [Southern] preachers and evangelists . . . did, and how they moved people. She could bring about mass hypnotism."

Fame soon followed and she began performing both blues and jazz in nightclubs. Wherever she would appear, the lines of people waiting to see her would snake around city blocks and cause near riots and traffic jams. Ultimately, she recorded over 150 disks, drawing on a great deal of black oral tradition for her music. This was partially why she achieved such fame among the African American community—she was the proud carrier of black cultural heritage. Indeed, more than any woman of her time, Bessie became a symbol of African American racial pride and an outspoken opponent of the unequal treatment and inferior status of blacks in the United States. She was also the highest paid African American entertainer of her day. At the peak of her fame in the twenties, she had a railroad car custom made for she and her troupe to travel in—thus helping her circumvent Jim Crow laws limiting the movement of blacks among whites.

Her life was full of the excesses and conflicts she often sang about. She married twice and had many lovers, both male and female. "She ate and drank with gusto and was especially fond of home-cooked southern food and moonshine," according to *Black Women in America*. A binge drinker, she was often violent when drunk and loved to prowl the seedier parts of town "where the funk was flying," as she put it.

When the Depression hit, declining sales caused Columbia records to drop her from the label; and her career went into a tailspin. In 1937, on her way to a gig that was supposed to be her comeback, she died in a car accident in Clarksdale, Mississippi. Ten thousand fans, friends, and mourners attended her funeral; and the country suffered an enormous loss never to be replaced in the blues world.

Other Southern Blues Greats

- **Miss Ida Cox,** born in 1896 in Taccoa, Georgia, wrote "Wild Women Don't have the Blues," which has subsequently become a feminist anthem.

- **Dinah Washington,** known as the Queen of the Blues, from Tuscaloosa, Alabama, was famous for an explosive temper as well as unstinting loyalty and generosity to friends, died in 1963 from an accidental overdose of sleeping pills.

- **Sippie Wallace** of Houston, Texas, was part of the Storyville scene in New Orleans at the birth of the 20th century and wrote songs "about what troubled me," including "Woman Be Wise, Don't Advertise Yo' Man" that later inspired contemporary musician Bonnie Raitt.

- **Big Maybelle,** born in Jackson, Tennessee, in 1924, was one of the first blues singers to adapt "the rhythms of southern-based blues to an urban landscape," as *Black Women in America* puts it, creating a style still known today as rhythm and blues. Her charted hits included "Candy" and "96 Tears."

- **Jessie Mae Hemphill,** from Como, Mississippi, worked all her life to preserve Mississippi blues. She was named Best Traditional Blues Artist in 1987 and 1988, and performs solo around the world with an electric guitar, fife and drums, and tambourine attached to her foot.

- Notorious **Nina Simone,** the smoky voiced chanteuse from Tryon, North Carolina—extremely popular in Europe—sings not only the blues, but wrote many civil rights protest songs in the '60s.

A Pearl of Great Price

*T*he oil refinery town of Port Arthur, Texas, may have been an unlikely birth place for rock's first female superstar, bad girl **Janis Joplin.** But it was on the Louisiana border; and Janis and the boys she ran with in high school in the '50s would make frequent forays into the neighboring state—called going "on the line." That's where the blues-mama-in-training was exposed to the sounds of Ma Rainey and Bessie Smith (for whom, in 1970, Janis bought a tombstone), as well as the raucous sounds of Gulf Coast bands such as the Boogie Kings. Single-handedly self-formed, Joplin was outrageous at a time when girls were supposed to be buttoned up *and* down. One of the guys she hung out with at the time remembered in her biography, *Buried Alive,* "It was unheard of for a woman to yell, 'Well, f@%# you, baby!' It even embarrassed *us.*" But with unruly hair, acne scars and a tendency to be pudgy, she also didn't fit anyone's notion of beauty, which was extremely difficult for her in the looks-conscious South. She ended up quitting the University of Texas at Austin, after being voted "Ugliest Man on Campus." She was "laughed . . . out of class, out of town, and out of the state," as she later told Dick Cavett. It was 1963.

At seventeen, the raw-voiced, emotional powerhouse began singing in clubs, doing drugs and drinking—Southern Comfort, of course, the drink that was so synonymous with her "that she even scammed a fur coat out of the company for 'promoting their product,'" reports the *Pearl Fanzine Website for Janis Joplin.* Three years later, in San Francisco, she became the "chick singer" for Big Brother and the Holding Company. The following year, she mesmerized the crowd at the Monterey Pop Festival, becoming so hot that the band broke up so that Janis could pursue a solo career. Fans literally clawed and bit to get tickets to her concerts. *Vogue* described her on stage in 1968 as "a

magnetic moving fireball lighting up the whole auditorium" and she was famous for wild, gyrating simulations of sex acts on stage. Her trademark songs included: "Piece of My Heart," "Ball and Chain," and "Me and Bobby McGee."

Lovers for a time with Kris Kristofferson and Country Joe McDonald, she continued to booze (and drug) it up and brawl. "She's like plugged-in sandpaper," said photographer Richard Avedon, after shooting her. "Maybe my audiences can enjoy my music more if they think I'm destroying myself," she once mused. In one famous incident, Janis and Jim Morrison got into a brawl; he slammed her head onto a coffee table; she retaliated by hitting him over the head with a bottle, then cackling over his prostrate body.

By October 1970, she was dead of an accidental heroin overdose in a Los Angeles hotel room (although rumors on the Internet include murder by an angry drug pusher, or by the FBI in an anti-rock conspiracy that is somehow related to the murder of John F. Kennedy—the theory is that rock stars with the initials J, F, and K were targeted). Perhaps she knew she would burn out early, for the twenty-seven year old left $2,500 to provide for her wake. At the service, the Grateful Dead played for the two hundred attendees, each of whom had received an invitation stating: "Drinks are on Pearl." Country Joe McDonald claimed in *Janis Joplin*, "Sexism killed her. Everybody wanted this sixties chick who sang real sexy and had a lot of energy . . . and people kept saying one of the things about her was that she was just 'one of the guys' . . . that's a real sexist bulls@%# trip, 'cause that was f@%#ing her head around."

Interest in the defiant woman often called "The Greatest White Woman Blues Singer" remains high. Several of her albums, including *Pearl*, were posthumously released to enormous success, and there have been at least nine biographies and four songs written about her. As of this writing, there are two movies in the works on her life—one starring singer Melissa Etheridge, whose rendition of "Piece of My Heart" accompanied Janis' induction into the Rock and Roll Hall of Fame.

66My music ain't supposed to make you want to riot! My music's supposed to make you want to f@%#!**99**
    —*Janis Joplin*

Singing for the Lord

The great **Mahalia Jackson,** hailed at one time by the white press as "the only Negro whom Negroes have made famous," was once approached by Louis Armstrong in the late 1930s. An admirer of her deep, dark contralto voice, he was trying to get her to sing the blues with his band. Mahalia no doubt could have done it, growing up in "N'awlins" in the teens and twenties, and cutting her teeth listening to Bessie Smith, Jelly Roll Morton, and Ida Cox. But this staunch Baptist had other plans—she had dedicated her voice to God and wasn't about to be tempted by fame or fortune in giving up the gospel (although in 1958, she did record Duke Ellington's "Come Sunday" and "Black, Brown, and Beige" with the Ellington orchestra). Besides, she once said, "When you sing gospel, you have a feeling there is a cure for what's wrong. But when you sing the blues, you've got nothing to rest on."

Born in a three-room shotgun shack, between the train tracks and the Mississippi River on Water Street in New Orleans, she was raised by her mother's sisters after her mother died when Mahalia was four. Singing in the church choir was the sole focus of her childhood; and she was baptized in the waters of the "mighty Mississippi" at twelve. In 1927, she moved to Chicago, joined the choir of the Greater Salem Baptist Church, and became its lead singer. A year later, she became a member of the Johnson Gospel Singers, touring the southern and midwestern states, singing a new style of music: a blend of jazz, blues, spirituals, field hollers, hand clapping, and foot stomping, considered by many Southern Baptists as "the devil's music." "She said she had to praise God with her whole body," notes *Black Women in America*, "and she did," despite the stinging criticism that she lacked dignity. But she also had to keep body and soul together and a roof over her head, so she opened a beauty parlor after studying cosmetology at fellow belle Madame C. J. Walker's beauty school.

She also teamed up with Thomas Dorsey, the so-called Father of Gospel Music, who was largely responsible for the spread of gospel through his work as a composer—he penned over 400 songs—and promoter. He recognized in Mahalia a powerful instrument for his music and guided her career for over a decade, as she performed many of his songs and recorded with him. Largely due to her influence, gospel singing began to gain respectability.

In 1947, at the age of thirty-six, she was named the soloist with the National Baptist Convention and recorded "Move On Up a Little Higher" which sold more than two million copies in one year and eight million altogether during her lifetime. No more cutting hair! She recorded seven other hymns that would achieve sales of over one million copies, including "I Believe," "I Can Put My Trust in Jesus" and "He's Got the Whole World in His Hands." By the early '50s, she was crowned the undisputed queen of gospel music. She had her own radio program, appeared on Ed Sullivan's and Dinah Shore's television shows, as well as in several movies, and toured Europe to sell-out crowds (and twenty-one curtain calls in Paris). And it was standing room only when she appeared at Carnegie Hall in 1954 and at the Newport Jazz Festival in 1958.

She was busy in the early '60s too. Performing at one of the inaugural parties for John F. Kennedy, she and her powerful voice were also at the March on Washington in 1963 where she sang "We Shall Overcome." And she belted out "How I Got Over" just before Martin Luther King, Jr. gave his famous "I Have a Dream" speech, becoming one of the most potent symbols for civil rights. An eighth grade dropout, she established a scholarship fund to help young adults receive a college education. When she died in 1972, she had funerals in New Orleans and Chicago and is buried in Metairie, Louisiana.

❝I'm just a good strong Louisiana woman who can cook rice so every grain stands by itself.**❞**

—*Mahalia Jackson*

Voices Like "Farm-Fresh Honey"

$\mathcal{D}$iana Ellen Judd was only eighteen years old when she gave birth to Christina Claire Ciminella in 1964 in Ashland, Kentucky. Theirs was a life lived on and off the road in Kentucky, northern California, and Hollywood, as Mama alternately worked as a nurse, movie extra (renting her red and white '57 Chevy to the producers of *American Graffiti* and landing a bit part), model (appearing on the jacket of Conway Twitty's album, *Lost in the Feeling*), and one time secretary to the '60s singing group, The Fifth Dimension. Meanwhile, daughter Christina taught herself to play guitar and the two would sing together for fun. Landing back in Kentucky after Diana's divorce, they renamed themselves **Naomi and Wynonna Judd** and one day, "while nursing the daughter of top producer Brent Maher," reports Andrew Vaughn in *Who's Who in New Country Music*, "took the opportunity of passing on a cheaply made demo tape" recorded on a cassette player bought at K-Mart.

Faster than you could say superstars, the mother-daughter duo burst on the country music scene in 1984, with two back-to-back number one hits, "Why Not Me?" and "Mama, He's Crazy." "You heard about an overnight success? We were a coffee-break success. It happened that fast," recalls Naomi in her autobiography, *Love Can Build a Bridge*, which was also the name of their 1991 megahit album which sold one million copies, went platinum almost overnight, and won two Grammy Awards. Between 1988 to 1991, they won the County Music Vocal Duo of the Year four times running.

Naomi, who is now married to Larry Strickland, retired from singing in 1991, because of chronic hepatitis, which is currently in remission. "If y'all don't believe in God," she said about that, "you're a few sandwiches short of a picnic." She's recently done several guest appearances on television shows including *The Client* and *3rd Rock*

From the Sun. And of her life she says, "I made my mistakes when I was a teenager. I got married when I was seventeen—you can't top that one."

Wynonna continues to record successfully on her own (solo hits include "Tell Me Why" and "No One Else on Earth"), although initially she struggled; when the duo had performed together, she was the "shy youngster who anchored the music. Naomi was the outgoing Southern Belle that made the stage show sparkle," as a reporter for the University of Texas put it. Wynonna, herself, says of her transformation: "The first album was—I'm moving away from home but I'm still going back for meals. With [the second] album—I've got my own apartment, it's all furnished and I'm staying up real late." She recently married the father of her two children, Nashville businessman Arch Kelley III. The reception was held at Naomi's Nashville restaurant, Trilogy; and sister Ashley crashed the bridal chamber at the Opryland Hotel to croon "Goodnight Irene." Along with stardom has come the obligatory negative press; and, in 1996, a former farm hand for the newly-married couple sued them, claiming Wynonna asked her to massage her buttocks and Arch tried to measure her butt.

    66I'm divorced and I've been to the circus and seen the clowns. This ain't my first rodeo.**99**

      —Naomi Judd (with a heavy debt to Joan Crawford)

    66How many times can you reinvent yourself? How many darn hair colors do you have to be? . . . I've tried just about every darn thing I can try and . . . it's time to get off [my] butt and stop complaining.**99**

      — Wynonna Judd

Like Mother, Like Other Daughter

Respected young actress **Ashley Judd** (*Ruby in Paradise, Smoke,* and *A Time to Kill*), whose mother once referred to her as an "intellectual pin-up," has gotten a lot of press about what she does or does not wear. That's because in 1995, the youngest daughter of Naomi Judd, who was still in school when her mother and sister hit the big time (attending twelve schools in thirteen years), told talk show host and fellow belle Oprah Winfrey, on air, that she doesn't wear underpants. Linked romantically with Lyle Lovett, Matthew McConaughey, and Michael Bolton, the smoldering Southern beauty, who smoked cigars before it was trendy, 'cause she was "a Kentuckian," likes to "fry chicken or make biscuits and gravy" in her spare time.

THIS GAL'S GOT LEGS!

*I*n the '60s and early '70s, when **Tina Turner** used to strut her stuff on stage with the Ike and Tina Turner Review, belting out tunes like "I Want to Take You Higher" and "Proud Mary," little did anyone suspect that she was an abused wife, who once had even attempted suicide. Now, after the publication of her autobiography (with former *Rolling Stone* and current MTV news reporter Kurt Loder), *I, Tina*, and the 1993 hit move based on her life, *What's Love Got to Do With It?*, the whole world knows the story of Anna Mae Bullock from Nutbush, Tennessee.

A sharecropper's daughter raised by her grandmother, Anna Mae met Ike Turner in 1956, when she was still in high school. She and her sister had gone to see his show and he had picked her out of the audience to sing with him. Needless to say, he was impressed with her golden pipes. He changed her name to Tina, and, when she got pregnant by his saxophone player, urged her to move in with him and his wife. Soon, however, the wife was out and Tina was in; and the two eventually married and had a baby. For twenty years, they lived and worked together, hitting international stardom when they opened for the Rolling Stones in 1969. (Mick Jagger is reputed to have learned his on-stage gyrations from Tina, a story that she downplays.) Privately, however, her life was hell, with Ike controlling everything down to what she wore and who she talked to.

Finally, in 1975, Tina, with the help of Buddhist chanting, had enough of Ike's domination and walked out with 36¢ in her pocket, determined to live life her way. Living on food stamps, she began playing small clubs, where she had a huge following among drag queens. "They were fabulous," she remembers, "They all dressed like me and knew all the words to my songs, they were so over the top." On her life with Ike, in her autobiography, *I, Tina*, she says, "I always like to say that I graduated from the Ike

Turner Academy, and that I took care of all my homework before I left him."

Nine years later, she was back on top with the album *Private Dancer* that sold 26 million copies worldwide and brought her four Grammys, including Record of the Year,

Best Pop Vocal Performance, Best Contemporary Rock Vocal Performance, and Song of the Year, for a remake of Al Green's "What's Love Got to Do With It?" (a song Tina didn't like at first because it was too tame). Since then, the woman dubbed "The Comeback Queen" has appeared in several movies, including *Mad Max Beyond Thunderdome* and did a scary cult classic turn in the Who's *Tommy,* as the Acid Queen. She has had several other subsequent hit albums and record-breaking world tours, playing to 7.5 million people in the 1990s alone. She is particularly popular in Europe—her greatest hits album, *Simply the Best,* stayed in the British top fifty for three years—where she lives with her German boyfriend.

Currently fifty-eight and still performing in teeny-tiny skirts that show off her great legs (and doing advertising for Hanes hosiery), wearing high, high heels, red lips, and her trademark wig, the fabulous looking

grandmother maintains her looks are completely natural. "There's not a piece of plastic in me," she claims, although she does admit to having her breasts lifted after her second son was born thirty years ago. "I love being a woman," she commented in her autobiography. "I love every oil, every cream, every bottle of perfume, anything made for women." Although she leads a quiet life off stage, she admits to still being wild on stage because that's how she feels: "I will never give into old age until I *become* old. And I am *not old yet*."

66I'm a southern girl. We have mud on our feet.**99**
— *Tina Turner*

6.

Bar Belles:
Astounding Athletes

They ran, jumped, threw, and pumped, and were so good at it that they made their way into record books, Olympic fame, and worldwide acclaim. True Southerners—ain't nothin' sissy about these gals.

ALL THAT AND A COCA-COLA

*R*unning and jumping was **Alice Coachman's** business; and she did it so well there is now a street in Tuskegee, Alabama, named just for her — Alice Avenue — as well as a school — Coachman Elementary. As a child in rural Albany, Georgia, in the 1920s, however, she was just a little black girl who would practice the high jump by tying rags together between two trees on a dirt road and hurling herself over them. One day, a man saw her and said to her mother, "that gal's going to jump over the moon one of these days." Not quite, but in 1948, she did make history, becoming the first African American to win an Olympic medal. Alice, going full steam all the way, followed her heart and captured the gold in the high jump.

Alice was the fifth of ten children, in a household ruled by her father, a plasterer who would whip her whenever she left the house to go run, because he wanted his daughters to be "dainty, sitting on the front porch" when they weren't cooking and cleaning. But Alice had other ideas — she would chase after boys "to give me competition,"she told *The Atlanta Journal-Constitution* in 1995. "They dared not say anything out of the way or even touch me because I would beat up on them." She broke the AAU high school and college women's high jump records while barefoot, and was recruited on a working scholarship by Tuskegee Institute, which had become a training ground for women runners. While in college, in addition to winning an amazing twenty-six national titles in both the high jump and 50-meter dash, Alice sang in the school choir, performed with the drill team, and worked her way through school cleaning the pool and gym, sewing football uniforms, and rolling the clay tennis courts. Oh, and in her ample free time, she played soccer, field hockey, volleyball, and basketball (as a guard, she led the Tuskegee team to three consecutive conference championships). "I just wanted to win," she humbly told the *Albany Herald* in 1984.

Originally, she was supposed to compete in the 1940 Olympics, which were canceled due to World War II. Ditto again in 1944. Finally, in 1948, the Games were on again, but Alice was sick and thought to be past her prime. She ultimately decided to compete because "I didn't want to let my country down, or my family and school. Everyone was pushing me, but they knew how stubborn and mean I was, so it was only so far they could push me." At the Games, she watched dejectedly as her teammates lost race

after race, until Alice was the only one left. She led them to Olympic glory.

After her win, she became the first black woman to endorse an international product, Coca-Cola, appearing on billboards across the country with 1936 Olympic hero, Jesse Owens. Her victory cleared the way for African American women, who since that time have come to dominate U.S. track and field.

Alice went on to become a coach and a teacher, and was inducted into the National Track and Field Hall of Fame in 1975. After retirement, she used her fame and notoriety to found the Alice Coachman Track and Field Foundation to help both children and retired athletes.

❝That ain't the half of it, honey, but that's all I'm telling.**❞**
—*Alice Coachman*

GOLDEN GIRL

Alice isn't the only famous southern runner, not by a mile. Another woman worthy of mention is Georgian **Wyomia Tyus,** who as a child was stricken with polio and wore corrective shoes until she was ten. A mere eight years later, she

won a gold medal in the 100-meter dash at the Tokyo Olympics. At the 1968 Mexico City Olympics, she became (at the time) one of only two women ever to win three gold medals and earned a place in the Olympic Hall of Fame. Her appearance there was controversial — militants had encouraged black athletes to boycott the games. However, Wyomia, a true rebel belle not wanting to miss the opportunity of a lifetime, went and fortuitously won, but wore black clothing in support.

Most Valuable Player

In her prime, she was so famous she was known simply as Babe. That's because Texan **Babe** (real name: Mildred) **Didrikson Zaharias** was one of the greatest natural athletes of all time. She could run, high jump, throw the javelin, play pool, swim, shoot some mean hoops and swing a hot bat. A little wisp of a gal who stood just five-foot-four and barely weighed over 100 pounds, in the 1932 Olympics, she won the hearts of the American public by taking gold medals in the 80-meter hurdles and the javelin. And, as Charles McGrath points out in a 1996 profile in *The New York Times Magazine*, "She would have won the high jump too, if the judges hadn't objected to her controversial technique of diving headfirst over the bar."

And then there was her golf game. Determined to make money at athletics — times were different in the '30s, there were no big athletic shoe or cereal box contracts for Olympic stars, and money was tight in her working-class family (as a junior high school student, Babe had worked in a fig-packing plant and later sewed potato sacks), Babe decided to go where a woman could make money as an athlete and became a professional golfer. She applied her usual grit to succeeding; practicing until her hands were raw, she would often bandage them and continue on. While she perfected her technique, Babe kept body and soul together by various means, including playing on several women's baseball teams and doing vaudeville (she tumbled and played the harmonica).

Then she hit the women's golf circuit, dominating the sport throughout the '30s and '40s. She won seventeen straight amateur victories in one year, a record yet to be broken by either a man or woman, and won thirty-three pro tournaments, including three U.S. Opens. She won the Associated Press' Woman Athlete of the Year five times and in 1950, was named the AP's Outstanding Woman Athlete of the Half Century.

Co-founder of the Ladies Pro Golf Association (LPGA) in 1949, she brought an athleticism to the sport that had for women been formerly characterized by elegant, but not very powerful, shots. Babe wasn't concerned about being ladylike. "It's not enough to swing at the ball," she once said. "You've got to loosen your girdle and really let the ball have it." She often played in exhibition matches against men; and, in 1951, she took up a challenge by British golf journalist Leonard Crawley who, skeptical about the abilities of female pro golfers, bet Babe that she and her compadres couldn't beat the best six male amateur golfers in the world. If they did, Leonard would shave off his moustache. Babe, in typical belle fashion, rose to the challenge; and the women swept every match. Leonard, however, kept his moustache.

In 1938, she married wrestler George Zaharias, nicknamed "The Crying Greek from Cripple Creek," who managed her career. Perhaps her finest moment was in 1954, when she amazed the world by winning the U.S. Open by twelve strokes, less than a year after undergoing major abdominal surgery for intestinal cancer. The cancer eventually stopped her, however; and her death, at the age of forty-three in 1956, was a huge loss for the sports world and all of America.

66I always knew what I wanted to be when I grew up. My goal was to be the greatest athlete who ever lived.**99**
— *Babe Didrikson Zaharias*

PUMPING IRON

*R*achel **Livia Elizondo McLish** didn't set out to make weight lifting an acceptable women's activity; but that's just what the Texas native did by bringing glamour to women's bodybuilding. As a girl growing up in the early '60s, she was more drawn to the "feminine" sports, studying ballet and dreaming of becoming a dancer. But she was always fascinated by her father's weight lifting regimen. In high school, she fell for that female siren call, cheerleading, with its promise of dates and popularity and gave up ballet—there just wasn't time for both. But, by the time she went to Pan American University in 1974, she already regretted her choice. The years away from practice made a return to ballet impossible.

But she decided to do *something* physical, and began lifting weights at a health club (weights were not popular then and were hard to find), working her way through school and paying club membership dues by teaching exercise classes and later by managing the club. Upon graduating with a degree in health and physical education, she and some partners founded the Sport Palace, the first health spa in south Texas, soon to be followed in rapid succession by two other successful branches. It was at this time that Rachel heard about the first ever, U.S. women's bodybuilding championship, to be held in 1980. She decided to compete because it was a good advertisement for her club; and she wanted to prove you didn't have to look like a man to be a bodybuilder. She won the title, went on to win three other championships, and began to appear in women's magazines and on the lecture circuit, discussing women's health, fitness, and beauty.

Much to her credit, women now routinely use weight training in their fitness programs. But Rachel walked away from competition when it began to emphasize muscular development; and many competitors began to abuse steroids to build bulk and definition.

She has written several books on fitness and health, appeared on television programs and in movies, and in 1990, even launched a line of activewear for K-Mart. "The point of physical fitness is not narcissism or egotism," she said in an interview with the *Los Angeles Times*. "It's well-being. Most people don't know what it's like to feel good all over."

TOTAL KNOCK OUT

Hessie Donahue was just trying to be a good wife. So in 1892, when her husband, a boxing promoter, was at an exhibition in Arkansas promoting legendary fighter John L. Sullivan, and there were no volunteers to do a little sparring, Hessie agreed to climb into the ring. However, John tagged Hessie's nose a little too hard. She got mad, hauled off and belted him; and down he went for the count. Making Hessie the only woman to ever knock out a major boxing champion—at least in the ring.

Hoop Queen

As a girl, **Lusia Harris-Stewart** dared to dream the dream of so many young black boys: to be a basketball superstar. Never mind that she was a girl and there were no professional women's teams at the time; basketball was her life—and she was just about better than anyone.

Born in 1955, the seventh of nine children on a vegetable farm in Minter City, Mississippi (population 200), Lusia first shot hoops with her brothers and sisters, then took to the backboards of her junior high and high school. Recruited by a small, previously unknown white college, Delta State University in Cleveland, Mississippi, she led her team to three Association of Intercollegiate Athletics for Women (AIAW) Basketball Championships in 1975, '76 and '77.

During the mid-'70s, she dominated women's basketball; and the number of awards she won is mind boggling. The six-foot-three-inch center was the high scorer at the 1976 Olympics, the first time women's basketball was an Olympic sport, with Lusia scoring the first two points in Olympic women's basketball history and leading her team to a silver medal. She was also top scorer at the 1975 World Games and Pan American Games. She was selected three times to the Kodak All-American team, the AIAW All-Tournament team, and was voted most valuable player at the AIAW National Championship in 1976. That same year, she was proclaimed Mississippi's first Amateur Athlete of the Year. She was in the midst of a three-year, fifty game winning streak when she performed as part of a women's team that played Madison Square Garden and led her team to victory with forty-seven points. In 1977, she won the Broderick Award for the top basketball player in the AIAW and the Broderick Cup for outstanding female collegiate athlete.

She won all these awards while attending school full time and being a campus leader. And to top it off, she also became the first black woman at Delta State to be chosen homecoming queen.

But life wasn't all successes for the basketball star. She was the only African American player on her team and one of only a handful of black players at the time on women's collegiate teams. Notes *Black Women in America*, "she served as a lonely superstar role model for Black girls and women." And after college, there was nowhere for her to display her awesome talent, at least certainly not for the salaries that her male peers would command. In 1980, she played for a brief time in the Women's Pro League, but she was past her prime and the league was ultimately short lived. She married George Stewart, had four sons, and now teaches physical education and coaches women's basketball. In May, 1992, she was one of the first two women inducted into the Springfield Basketball Hall of Fame.

YOU'RE OUT!

Pitcher **Jackie Mitchell** was the first woman to sign with a pro baseball team. In April 1931, she was pitching for Chattanooga against the Yankees and struck out both the legendary Babe Ruth and equally famous Lou Gehrig back to back.

NO PRESSURE TOO GREAT

*W*ho alive in 1984 can forget the image of pixie-like **Mary Lou Retton** at the Summer Olympics? Her lithesome body, perky good looks, and spunky spirit left an indelible mark on the American consciousness. (Plus, who could forget the face you saw for years on your Wheaties box?) Mary Lou was so popular that in 1993, nine years after the Olympics in which she won five medals in gymnastics, including the gold for all around excellence, silver in team and vault, and bronze in uneven bars and floor exercise, she was still picked as the most popular female athlete in America (sharing the honors with iceskater Dorothy Hamill).

Mary Lou was born in a small coal mining town in West Virginia, the youngest of five. By age four, she was already enrolled in acrobatic and ballet classes, something her parents did because she was "very hyper." By seven, she was already training seriously; at eight, she saw Nadia Comaneci in the Olympics and began to plan for her own equal success. At fifteen, she moved to Houston to train with Bela Karolyi, the man who had coached Nadia and began to win major prizes.

One of Mary Lou's great skills, besides her pure athleticism, was her ability to convey her warm, sunny, down-home disposition, which endeared her to all who watched the little (four foot-nine-inch) ball of energy. Don Peters, the U.S. women's gymnastics team

coach told the *New York Times* about the then sixteen year old, "Mary Lou has two great qualities that put her where she is. First, physically, she is the most powerful gymnast who ever competed in the sport and she takes great advantage of that in her tumbling and her vaulting . . . Second, she's one hell of a competitor. As the pressure gets greater, Mary Lou gets greater."

Just six weeks before she was to appear in the Olympics, she injured her knee and had to have arthroscopic surgery; but, by competition time, she seemed to have totally recovered when she took to the arena and charmed the world. That year, in addition to her medals (and the Wheaties box), she was named *Sports Illustrated* Sportswoman of the Year and toured twenty-eight cities in the U.S., performing and appearing in parades. Still sought after for sports telecasting, product endorsements, and exhibitions, she lives in Houston, where she is married and has a child. She also gives inspirational speeches: "I tell people how to leave the comfort zone and meet life's challenges." Spoken like a true hell's belle.

FORE!

In 1926, miniature golf was invented by a Tennessee entrepreneur **Frieda Carter,** part owner of the Fairyland Inn, who called it "Tom Thumb Golf" when she applied for a patent. Growing by leaps and bounds, in 1930 there were 50,000 such courses nationwide.

THE FASTEST WOMAN ON EARTH

*W*ilma **Rudolph** was just a little girl of four in Bethlehem, Tennessee, in 1959, when she contracted scarlet fever and polio, which left her with a useless leg. Her family's circumstances were dire—her father had eleven children by a previous marriage and eight with Wilma's mother. He worked as a porter for the railroad and her mother cleaned houses six days a week; so care for little Wilma's leg was not a top priority; survival was. But two years later, she began physical therapy, riding fifty miles twice a week to Nashville in the back of the segregated bus with her mother for five straight years in a row. By eleven, she stunned physical therapists who predicted she would always be disabled, by walking without braces; and, "by the time I was twelve," she once told the *Chicago Tribune*, "I was challenging every boy in the neighborhood at running, jumping, everything."

When she was in high school, where she won every race she ran, a coach from Tennessee State University saw her and started her training in earnest. Wilma didn't even know what the Olympics were; but she soon caught on, winning the bronze medal in the 1956 Games in the 4x100-meter relay at age sixteen, while still in high school. The win whetted her appetite for greater glory; and she determined to come back with a gold in 1960.

That she did—and then some. She won three gold medals—in the 100-meter dash, 200-meter dash, and 4x100-meter relay, becoming the first American woman to win three gold medals in track and field in a single Olympics. The French dubbed her, *"La Gazelle,"* and the Americans, "The Fastest Woman on Earth." But despite her fame—she was given ticker tape parades (including one in her hometown of Clarksville, Tennessee, for which 40,000 people turned out for the first integrated event in the town's history),

was invited by President Kennedy to the White House, and was asked to appear on all kinds of television programs—she saw little financial gain. Such exposure without the dollars to back it up was hard, a matter she acknowledged years later in an interview in *Ebony* magazine: "You become world famous and you sit with kings and queens, and then your first job is just a job. You can't go back to living the way you did before because you've been taken out of one setting and shown the other. That becomes a struggle and makes *you* struggle."

In 1961, she set a new world record, running the 100-meter dash in 11.2 seconds. But she decided to skip the 1964 Games, fearful that she could not duplicate her performance, and retired from athletics to go back to school. She graduated from Tennessee State University in 1963 (where she had worked her way through school doing jobs around campus) and became a second grade teacher at the elementary school she had attended. Later she worked for the Job Corps and Operation Champion, a 1967 program to bring star athletes into U.S. ghettos to inspire kids; she always loved speaking to young people about the value of athletics. Obviously they appreciated her attention. "In 1991," notes *Epic Lives*, "puzzled and angered over the fact that there was no mention of

Rudolph in the World Book Encyclopedia, the fourth-grade class of Jessup Elementary School in Jessup, Maryland, wrote to the publisher to urge inclusion. World Book obliged, and its 1991 edition features an entry."

In 1977, she authored her autobiography entitled, *Wilma: The Story of Wilma Rudolph,* which was made into a television movie with Cicely Tyson. Inducted into both the Olympic Hall of Fame and the National Track and Field Hall of Fame, she died of brain cancer after being honored as one of "The Great Ones" at the first National Sports Awards in 1993.

❝The triumph can't be had without the struggle. And I know what struggle is. I have spent a lifetime trying to share what it has meant to be a woman first in the world of sports so that other young women will have a chance to reach their dreams.❞
— *Wilma Rudolph*

TOUGH AS NAILS

Now this may not be athletic, but it is certainly a feat of physical endurance. In 1809, forty-seven-year-old **Jane Todd Crawford,** in massive pain, rode sixty miles on horseback from Greensburg, Kentucky, to Danville, where she was operated on (remember, there was no anesthesia at the time) to remove a twenty-two and one-half pound ovarian tumor. Hers was the first successful such operation. She was up less than a week later, making her own bed, and lived for thirty-three more years.

OUT OF THE MOUTHS OF BELLES

66 Women in country music are either saints or sluts, but they are mostly sluts. She's either a 'good-hearted woman' or a 'honky-tonk angel.' There are more hard-hearted women in country music ('I Gave Her a Ring, She Gave Me the Finger'), despicable bimbos ('Ruby, Don't Take Your Love to Town'), and heartless gold diggers ('Satin Sheets to Lie On, Satin Pillow to Cry On') than the scholars can count. Even the great women country singers aren't much help. The immortal Patsy Cline was mostly lovesick for some worthless heel ('I Fall to Pieces') and Tammy Wynette's greatest contribution was to advise us 'Stand By Your Man.' (Tammy has stood by several.) 99

—*Molly Ivins*

66 Gossip is news running ahead of itself in a red satin dress. 99

—*Liz Smith*

66 I wanted to be the first woman to burn her bra, but it would've taken the fire department four days to put it out. 99

—*Dolly Parton*

166

66 If you had to work in the environment of Washington, D.C., as I do, and watch those men who are so imprisoned and so confined by their 18th-century thought patterns, you would know that if anybody is going to be liberated, it's men who must be liberated in this country. 99

> —*Barbara Jordan, speech, International Women's Year Conference, Austin, Texas, November 10, 1975.*

66 When I hear women talk about their jobs, all they say is him, him, him, and honey, this ain't church. 99

> —*Patsy Cline*

66 I'm supposed to have had more men than most people change their underwear. 99

> —*Tanya Tucker*

66 Really, that little dealybob is too far away from the hole. It should be built right in. 99

> —*Loretta Lynn, on the female anatomy*

7

Bellewethers
and
Bossy Belles

These women sure do know how to take charge in the proper southern manner—with a smile, of course.

Right Place, Right Time

*N*ew Orleans in the mid-1800s was really a place for free-thinking (and living) women. One was **Eliza Nicholson,** who became the first woman publisher of a major newspaper when she took over the *New Orleans Daily Picayune* in 1875. Like later publishing moguls, including Katherine Graham, she got the job through marriage, or more accurately, widowhood. Once in command, she started Dorothy Dix on her famous newspaper career, founded the Women's International Press Association in 1887, and hired many white women to work on the paper, including Fanny B. Ward, who was the only woman journalist to report on the sinking of the battleship *Maine* in the Spanish-American War. Although she was a strong advocate of women's rights, she was an incredible racist, opposing suffrage because it would give African American women the vote.

A published writer by the age of fourteen, **Miriam Follin** also became a journalist through marriage. In 1861, when her husband became editor of *Frank Leslie's Illustrated Newspaper*, Miriam took over *Leslie's Ladies Magazine.* She also took over Frank Leslie himself and for a decade lived with both her husband and her boss, until she was finally granted a divorce by reason of insanity (his, not hers). Then she married Frank and became a roving reporter. She loved a good story, particularly a juicy one, and once wrote about an opium den and a San Francisco brothel. Frank died in 1880; and, with his death, she inherited the newspaper along with seventeen lawsuits (apparently he wasn't a good money manager). But Miriam soon straightened that out and went on to hire a great many women writers during her ten-year tenure. Tired of the newspaper trade, she sold out and had a brief marriage with Oscar Wilde's alcoholic brother. When she died, she left $2 million to Carrie Chapman Catt for women's suffrage, although that was contested; and ultimately Carrie received less than half of the intended sum.

MISTRESS OF MAHOGANY HILL

$\mathcal{N}$ew Orleans was famous for leniency toward ladies of the night. Under a 1897 ordinance instigated by city alderman Sidney Story, two city blocks around Basin Street, named Storyville, were the proud location of over two dozen "sporting palaces." The most ornate was Mahogany Hill, a four-story marble mansion run by famed madam **Lulu White** who called herself the "Queen of the *Demi-Monde.*" Lulu's place boasted five parlors and fifteen bedrooms, all done in lavish furnishings. She was so powerful that her girls were never arrested and her $40,000 mansion was assessed at only $300.

But life before Storyville was established wasn't nearly so cushy for Lulu. Born a light-skinned black on a farm near Selma, Alabama (although in repudiating her heritage, she would claim she was born in the West Indies with "not a drop of Negro blood"), in pre-Storyville days she was arrested so often on prostitution, white slavery, and disorderly conduct charges that "bringing Lulu in" became a weekly event for New Orleans cops. But over time she was able to attract, one after another, an oil magnate, a railroad baron, and a department store heir, all of whom feathered her nest quite nicely—bankrolling the mansion and the police bribes.

In her heyday, she made quite a stir. Reputed to be not particularly beautiful, she did have quite a sense of style. Each evening she would descend the staircase of her mansion, "decked out in her gaudy display of diamonds, smiling her celebrated diamond-studded smile and singing her favorite song, 'When the Moon Shines,'" exclaims *Storyville, New Orleans*. "Attired in a bright red wig and an elaborate formal gown, she wore diamond rings on all her fingers (including thumbs), bracelets up both arms, a diamond necklace, a tiara, and an emerald alligator brooch on her chest."

By 1917, Lulu's—and Storyville's—salad days were over. Federal authorities shut down the brothels; and Lulu lost most of her money. A shrewd businesswoman, Lulu had seen the handwriting on the wall and had been looking to diversify beyond prostitution. She had a sense that the film industry was about to boom in Los Angeles and had planned to invest in both real estate and production companies. If her plan had succeeded, she would have become the owner of one of the largest studios in the world. She sent her lover to Los Angeles with over $150,000 in cash (a gargantuan amount in those days), but he absconded with her loot, never to be heard from again.

Nobody knows exactly what happened to her after that. The saddest account is that she died in a baggage car returning penniless to Selma.

STORYVILLE'S STRUMPETS

The ladies of the night who worked for Lulu and others were often flamboyant both in dress and moniker. *Storyville, New Orleans* offers the following list of names of women who practiced their crafts there: Flamin' Mamie, Crying Emma, Bucktown Bessie, Mary Meathouse, Gold Tooth Gussie, Big Butt Annie, Bird Leg Nora, Cole Eyed Laura, Yellow Gal, Black Sis, Big Bull Cora, Kidneyfoot Rella, Sugar Pie, Cherry Red, Tooth Rena, Snaggle Mouf Mary, Lily the Crip, Tenderloin Thelma, Three Finger Annie, Cold Blooded Carrie and Miss Thing.

A TALE OF TWO RANCHERS

*F*ormer Louisiana slave **Coincoin** was the long-time concubine of Claude Metoyer, with whom she had ten children and who had purchased her freedom for her in an attempt to stave off a clerical battle over their "scandalous alliance." So far, the story is not all that unusual; most black women who were free in the 18th century were deemed so due to a sexual alliance. But when Coincoin and Claude parted in 1786 because he was taking a legal (read: white) wife, he gave the forty-four-year-old freewoman and mother of fifteen a plot of land and a small annuity. Coincoin took it from there—becoming an expert at growing cotton, corn, and tobacco, and raising cattle. She made so much money, she was able to purchase a land grant of 640 acres from the Spanish government. Then she decided to do something important with her money. She resolved to buy the freedom of all her children and grandchildren—some with cash, others on credit—and traveled as far as Texas over the next two decades to negotiate with their owners. By the time she died at the age of seventy-four, she had sixteen slaves herself, over 800 acres of land—a fortune at the time for a person of any color—and was able to bequeath her descendants a hefty inheritance.

It is this inheritance for which Coincoin goes down in history, for her family built upon it to become the largest slave-owning people of color in the world, with nearly 20,000 acres of land, 500 slaves, and a dozen manor houses on Isle Brevelle in the Red River Valley. They even had the only non-white church (Catholic) operating a white mission.

Then there's **Henrietta Chamberlain King,** the Queen of Cows, who was the founder of the largest cattle ranch in the world. In 1886, this fifty-three-year-old white woman inherited a debt-ridden 600,000 Texas acres from her husband. Rather than wallowing in failure, Henrietta met the challenge, ran the spread with her son-in-law, and pioneered some of the earliest scientific techniques for beef production, including the development of hardy Santa Gertrudis cattle (a cross between a shorthorn and a Brahma), for which King Ranch is now famous.

An extremely shrewd businesswoman, Henrietta also induced a railroad to build a line through her property (thus eliminating the problem of getting the cattle to the slaughterhouses) and solved the problem of water (always an issue) by importing a new kind of well-drilling rig that tapped an artesian well. When she died in 1925 at the age of ninety-two, the ranch consisted of one million acres and she left an estate worth over $5 million. Today, the King Ranch has holdings not only in the U.S., but also in Brazil, Argentina, Venezuela, and Australia.

BLUE BELLE

The Carolinas were only a colony in 1740, when seventeen-year-old **Eliza Lucas Pinckney** took over the management of her father's 5,000-acre plantation. Dad was called away to Antigua on business, but before he left, counseled Eliza to try some new crops. She took him at his word, experimenting with several before hitting upon indigo, a seed used in blue dye, which soon became the Carolinas' second most vital export (rice being the first).

HAIR APPARENT

*M*adam **C. J. Walker,** the world's first self-made female millionaire, was an illiterate black woman born Sarah Breedlove on a Delta, Louisiana, plantation in 1867 and orphaned seven years later, who became a haircare industry pioneer, philanthropist, and political activist. In speaking to the 1912 National Negro Business League Foundation, she told her story this way, "I am a woman who came from the cotton fields of the South. I was promoted from there to the washtub. Then I was promoted to the cook kitchen, and from there I promoted myself into the business of manufacturing hair goods and preparations . . . I have built my factory on my own ground."

Working as a field hand from the time she could walk, she became a domestic by age ten in Vicksbury, married at fourteen, and, at nineteen, was a widow with a two-year-old daughter (her husband was rumored to have been killed by a lynch mob). To support the two of them, she began selling haircare products door to door. Soon she had the idea that she could develop her own line of products. Her renowned hair loss formula came to her in a dream in which, "a big black man appeared to me and told me what to mix up for my hair. Some of the remedy was grown in Africa, but I sent for it, mixed it, put it on my scalp, and in a few weeks, my hair was coming in faster than it had ever fallen out."

In July, 1905, with $1.05 in savings, she moved to Denver, married Charles Joseph Walker, a newspaper sales agent, and set up a mail-order operation. Charles designed the advertisements and Sarah the concoctions, which she first tried out on friends. Later divorcing, she started a beauty training school advocating hot combing. Often credited with inventing the steel straightening comb, it is more likely, claims *Black Women in America,* that she actually adapted French products to suit black women's hair. Part of the raging debate over whether black women should change their hair's texture, she claimed in 1919, "Right here let me correct the erroneous impression held by some that I claim to straighten the hair. I want the great masses of my people to take a greater pride in their personal appearance and to give their hair proper attention."

As her fame and fortune grew, she moved several times, ultimately living in New York, and criss-crossing the country developing a network of over 25,000 black women who worked as commissioned agents in her business. She also traveled to the Caribbean to expand her market and began a career as a philanthropist. When she gave $1,000 to the YMCA in Indianapolis, it was the largest gift ever given by an African American woman in U.S. history. She stressed economic independence for black women and hired many at all levels of her company: "I want to say to every Negro woman present, don't sit down and wait for the opportunities to come . . . Get up and make them!"

She became increasingly outspoken on political issues, helping plan the famous Negro Silent Protest Parade in 1917 in New York City to support anti-lynching legislation and gave generous contributions to the NAACP. When she died at age fifty-one, her daughter took over her empire.

❝I got myself a start by giving myself a start.**❞**
—*Madame C. J. Walker*

YOU CAN TAKE THAT TO THE BANK

*A*nother self-made Walker of note is **Maggie Lena Walker.** The daughter of former slaves born in 1875 in Virginia, by the age of twenty-seven, she was the first woman bank president in the United States. She had always been precocious. As a teen in the segregated Richmond school system, she organized a strike of her fellow students to protest the fact that white students graduated in a theater, while African Americans had to make due with a church. Originally a teacher, she studied business and accounting and went to work for the Independent Order of Saint Luke, a mutual aid charitable organization headquartered in Richmond that she had joined at age fourteen. She was incredibly successful, rising from Secretary of the Good Idea Council to Right Worthy Grand Secretary, a secretary/treasurer post she held for over thirty years, turning the organization into a multi-million dollar operation in just a few years.

Her financial success enabled her to think she could run a bank; it also helped her see the need for one. Blacks in need of home loans were not welcomed at white banks and had little experience saving money. She decided to change that, and started St. Luke's Penny Thrift Savings Bank in Richmond in 1903. It eventually evolved into the Consolidated Bank and Trust Company, with Maggie at the helm until her death in 1934. Thanks to this enterprising soul, many black businesses got loans, and, by 1920, over 600 families were able to purchase a home. To encourage savings, she provided children "with little cardboard penny boxes to help them amass the minimum amount required to open an account: one dollar," notes *The Book of African-American Women*.

Maggie's community involvement went way beyond the bank. She was the first president of the Council of Colored Women, and a member of the International Council of Women of the Darker Races and the National Association of Wage Earners, and co-founder of the Richmond NAACP. When she died, the obituary in the *Richmond News Leader* read in part: "Maggie Walker was the greatest of all Negro leaders in Richmond . . . [and] one of three or four of the ablest women her race ever produced. In America."

> **❝**I was not born with a silver spoon in my mouth: but instead, with a clothes basket upon my head.**❞**
> —*Maggie Lena Walker*

BLACK MARY

Born a slave in 1832 in Tennessee, **"Black Mary"** was as strong as a man, fast with a gun, and stood six feet tall. She smoked cigars until the day she died and received special permission to drink with men in saloons. She made a living hauling freight in Montana, then ran a restaurant, which failed because she gave away so much free food. In her sixties, she got a job driving a stagecoach for the U.S. Mail and in her seventies ran her own a laundry business (and decked a customer who had skipped out on her). When the business burned down in 1912, the town chipped in to help rebuild it.

MOTHER OF THE MODERN DAY COOKIE SELLER

*J*uliette **(Daisy) Gordon Low** was a lonely widow from Savannah, Georgia, who was at her vacation lodge in Scotland, when she met Lord Robert Baden-Powell and heard about his forming the Boy Scouts and his sister the Girl Guides. She thought it a wonderful idea for young girls to have such a body- and character-building experience, and was soon meeting at her lodge with seven girls every Saturday to drink tea and

teach them about flag history, knot tying, first aid, and knitting. Moving on to London, she formed two Girl Guide troops there before heading home to Savannah and her life's vocation as founder of the Girl Scouts of America.

On March 12, 1912, eight girls, including her niece Daisy Gordon, met at her house to start the first Girl Scout troop. (Daisy preferred the word "scout" to "guide" because she believed it had more American connotations to it.) A great believer in physical activity for girls, she concocted vaguely militaristic uniforms—originally black bloomers, white middy blouses and black stockings, later changing to blue serge and settling on the now-familiar green—and emphasized calisthenics, hiking, and basketball. (In strong opposition to such athleticism, Luther Gulick founded the Camp Fire Girls in which girls "dressed like what a white man thought of as demure Indian maidens," according to *The American Women's Almanac,* and sang "songs around a suitably domestic campfire.")

Within a year, the budding organization was so successful that it moved to its national headquarters in Washington, D.C.; and, until her death in 1927, the original den mother worked ceaselessly to build the organization. Daisy's Savannah home is now a historical monument with a Girl Scout museum visited by thousands of tourists each year.

GIVE THAT LADY A RAISE!

Dorothy Shaver, native of Center Point, Arkansas, became the highest paid woman in the country in 1945, when she was named president of Lord & Taylor for a salary of $110,000—though as *Life* magazine pointed out at the time, it was only a quarter of what was being paid to a man in a similar job. In 1946 and '47, she was named Outstanding Woman in Business by the Associated Press and later won awards from The American Woman's Association and the Society of New York Dress Designers. Dorothy earned the kudos, if not a huge salary, for her unstinting support of American fashion designers, bringing many to the attention of the world for the first time, and for increasing Lord & Taylor's sales and bottom line. Holding steady at $30 million when she took over, she shepherded their increase to $100 million by 1959, when she was felled by a stroke and died.

THE ANGEL OF MERCY

*N*othing could stop **Eartha Mary Magdalene White,** a Jacksonville, Florida, businesswoman and community leader who was known as the "Angel of Mercy" to thousands of poor, sick, and homeless Floridians. Even when she was confined to a wheelchair in her nineties, she remained active in social welfare work until her death at age ninety-seven in 1974.

The daughter of a black woman and a white man, she was adopted by ex-slaves who instilled in her a deep pride in being black; and, armed with this belief, she broke down many racial barriers, eventually founding an African American museum. Her adoptive mother, Clara White, also taught her to give to those in need, a value she would embody her whole life. In 1895, after completing her schooling, she joined the Oriental-American Opera Company, one of the first black opera companies. Within the year, she returned to Jacksonville to teach and work as a secretary at the Afro-American Life Insurance Company. During the great fire of 1901, she risked her life to save the company's records. A savvy businesswoman, for the next twenty-five years, she owned and ran a series of small businesses, including a general store, a dry good store, and a laundry, where, she claimed, she could "clean anything but a dirty conscience." She would build each business up and then sell it for a profit and start all over again. She also bought and sold real estate, using the money she made to fund her charitable work.

She was indefatigable. In addition to running her own businesses, for many years, she ran the only black orphanage in the state, helped create the Colored Citizen's Protection League in 1900, started the Colored Old Folks' Home in 1902, revived the Union Benevolent Association to help Civil War veterans, organized the Boys Improvement Club, and launched "Save 1,000 Boys from Juvenile Court," a drive to raise money for a youth center, which she ultimately ended up funding and running herself, until 1916 when she finally persuaded the city government to take it over. And for over fifty years, she taught Sunday school at the county prison. Additionally, she was the War Camp Community Services and Coordinator of Recreation in Savannah during World War I, the only woman invited to the Southeast War Camp Community Service Conference, and the only African American to attend a White House Council of National Defense meeting.

In 1928, she started the Clara White mission in honor of her adoptive mother, living there herself, and feeding over 2,500 people in one month alone. The mission spawned a number of other projects: a home for pregnant women, a child placement service, a community center, and a home for people with tuberculosis.

During World War II, she established and managed many Red Cross activities in a building she had donated to servicemen. In 1941, she was one of the organizers of a march on Washington to protest job discrimination against African Americans. In response to the proposed march, Franklin Delano Roosevelt banned discrimination in the federal government and established the Fair Employment Practices Committee. In 1967, when Eartha was ninety years old, the 120-bed Eartha M. White Nursing Home, started with her own funds, was completed. She acquired many accolades for her work, including the Lane Bryant Volunteer Award, the American Nursing Home Association Better Life Award, and the National Negro League's Booker T. Washington Symbol of Service Award.

SHE'S THE BOSS

*A*rguably one of the most powerful women in business, and certainly one of the richest, (*Forbes* magazine included her on its annual list of the 400 Richest People in America), **Martha Ingram** came upon her fortune and position in 1995 when her husband, Bronson Ingram, died and left her Ingram Industries, a distribution company grossing, at the time, close to $12 billion.

Her previous business experience was in running Ingram's public affairs, choosing which charity and civic organizations the company would donate to, and starting the Tennessee Performing Arts Center—by convincing the state legislature to fork over $36 million—as well as the Tennessee Repertory Theater and the Nashville Ballet. But, notes Phil Phiffer, former executive vice president of Ingram in an article in *Computer Reseller News*, "She was elected chairman of the company because she was the person best qualified for the job. It was never a case in which she was elected because she was the widow."

The Charleston, South Carolina native, who is now a resident of Nashville, lost no time in taking the helm. First, she split the company into three-parts and appointed her three sons the head of one company each. She then was instrumental in picking a new CEO for Ingram Micro, a subsidiary that is the world's largest computer distributor, contributing two thirds of the revenue to Ingram's bottom line.

A woman in a decidedly male-dominated world, "Martha was really a belle, a Southern belle," remarked her sister Elizabeth Lewine, also in *Computer Reseller News*, who additionally noted that when they were kids, "after Martha had spent her allowance, she would borrow mine." No need to borrow from sis anymore; *Forbes* estimates her family's worth at $2 billion. However, Martha still won't take her husband's seat at the board of directors' table (his chair stands empty) and she can't bring herself to move into his office.

> 66 I don't want to hear about why it won't work. I want to hear about how it CAN work. 99
> *—Martha Ingram*

LIQUID GOLD

In 1956, divorcee **Bette Claire Nesmith,** a working mother and executive secretary, was sitting around her kitchen table in Dallas, trying to figure out how to fix a typing mistake instead of having to re-type the whole page, when she hit on the idea for Liquid Paper: tempera waterbased paint in a bottle with a little brush. (She called it Mistake Out originally.) She tried to sell the idea to IBM; but, lucky for her, they turned her down. She began bottling the stuff in her garage and was selling over one hundred bottles per month in her spare time, when she was fired from her job for typing "The Liquid Paper Company" instead of her employer's name on a letter. Eventually she turned the idea into a stationery-products giant producing 25 million bottles a year. Because of her sensitivity to women's issues, one of the subsidiaries of her firm was founded to offer childcare to working parents. She headed the company until 1975, when she sold it to Gillette for $47.5 million. (A timely sale indeed for the increased use of computers ultimately dried up the once enormous correction fluid market.)

SHE'D A DONE THE KING PROUD

*P*riscilla "Cilla" Beaulieu Presley is known, first and foremost, as Elvis' only wife. But in the last twenty-four years since their divorce, she has also made a name for herself as an actress (the *Naked Gun* series and *Dallas* being the most well-known). But the identity she has perhaps been most successful at, though least known for, is as a businesswoman. She comes by this designation, says Dotson Rader in a *Parade* article, by "virtually single-handedly saving from financial ruin the Presley estate and the inheritance of her daughter Lisa Marie." She did this by judicious sales of music and merchandising rights to Elvis' image and music, and by opening Graceland to the public. (It is now the second most visited residence in the U.S., for a fee of course, with a profitable gift shop, second only to the White House.) By virtue of Priscilla's smarts, Elvis' estate, worth around $4 million when he died, is currently estimated to be worth $100 million. Now that's playing your cards (or is it his tunes?) right. And in her spare time, she is a cosmetics scion, having just launched her third perfume, called Indian Summer.

Priscilla's early life gave no indication of her latent financial talents. Born in 1945 into a military family, her father died in a plane crash just after she was born. Her mother subsequently married another military man and they moved around a lot. Her stepfather was very strict, recalls Priscilla in her autobiography *Elvis and Me*, but she was clever. "When he refused to let me wear a tight skirt, I joined the Girl Scouts specifically so I could wear their tight uniform." When she was fourteen, she was crowned the Queen of Del Valley Junior High in Austin, Texas; but, that same day, her stepfather was transferred to Wiesbaden, Germany, taking the family with him. Having heard that Elvis was stationed forty-five minutes away, she finagled an invitation to a party at his house.

The rest is, as they say, history. The twenty-four-year-old singing sensation fell head over heels in love and, after three years, convinced Priscilla's parents to let her live with him (under the watchful eye of his grandmother) while she went to high school. "I was leading a double life—a schoolgirl by day, a femme fatale by night," she remarks in her autobiography. He dictated what she wore (form fitting), the kind of makeup (lots!) even the color (black) and style (big) of her hair; when her parents came to visit her stepfather exclaimed that her eyes looked like "two pissholes in the snow." She began to imitate Elvis' drug-taking habits; after all it was hard to go out on the town all night and get up for classes at 8 A.M. However, Priscilla, nicknamed "Toughie" by Elvis because she once threw a pillow at him and hurt him, maintains that, despite their living together, she remained a virgin until their wedding night four years later: "He was extremely protective of me, a real Southern gentleman."

Six years and one child later they were divorced. In a certain way, she was a young adult leaving home for the first time to find herself. By dictating how she would live and what she would look like, Elvis had made himself a parental figure to rebel against. She threw herself into fashion design and ran a boutique in Los Angeles for four years. But when Elvis died, she stepped in to save her daughter Lisa Marie's inheritance. She currently lives with long-time lover Marco Garibaldi, with whom she has one son, continues to act, and oversees the famous Elvis empire.

LIBERTY BELLE

One of the most prominent black women of the 20th century was **Mary McLeod Bethune,** the seventeenth child of former slaves. Born in 1875 in Mayesville, South Carolina, she realized the importance of education at age twelve, when she left home to attend the integrated Scotia Seminary in North Carolina on a scholarship from a Quaker in Denver. Upon graduation, she received another scholarship to Moody Bible College in Chicago, where her respect for education, particularly for African Americans, continued to grow.

In 1904, armed with only $1.50, she moved to Daytona, Florida, and founded the Daytona Educational and Industrial School for Training Negro Girls. It had five girls and one boy, her son, the product of a short-lived marriage to Albertus Bethune. She was a terrific businesswoman and a tireless fundraiser, securing funds from both Proctor & Gamble and J.D. Rockefeller. She excelled at scrimping and saving; in fact, the students picked elderberries to make ink and used burnt wood for chalk, while Mary bartered food for tuition and scavenged at the city dump for furnishings. By 1922, the school boasted three hundred students—all in uniforms to mask disparities in status—a dormitory, hospital, several class buildings, and a farm where students grew food. In 1929, the school merged with the Cookman Institute and became Bethune-Cookman College, which ultimately became accredited as a four year college and dropped its high school and elementary school. Mary stayed on as president until 1942, using her powerful oratory skills to raise money for the college throughout the North and receiving a great deal of support from liberal white Daytonans.

Originally she wanted to be a missionary; and this magnetic personality turned all of her missionary zeal into advancing the cause of African Americans, particularly women.

In the '20s, despite threats from the Klu Klux Klan, she led a successful voter drive to register black women, who'd recently received the vote. She led the fight to open a facility for wayward girls in Ocala; and, when she became concerned about blacks being turned away from Daytona hospitals, she helped found a hospital that trained black nurses. She was also the founder and president of the National Association of Colored Women and the National Council of Negro Women, where she met and became friends with Eleanor Roosevelt. That friendship led her to becoming a member of the Federal Council of Negro Affairs, often known as President Roosevelt's "Black Cabinet" which educated the Roosevelts to the problems of African Americans in the U.S.; Mary was the Cabinet's mother superior. Her role in Washington became so prominent that she ultimately gave up her college presidency.

One of the positions she held was Director of the Office of Minority Affairs of the National Youth Administration for which she traveled thousands of miles, to meet with African Americans, Chicanos, and Native Americans, to help them set up schools and minority training programs. In 1945, she was appointed by President Truman to represent the National Council of Negro Women at the founding sessions of the United Nations, the only non-white woman at the conference with official status. In 1952, three years before she died at the age of eighty, she founded the Central Life Insurance Company, to provide insurance to blacks, and became the only woman president of a national insurance company in the United States.

When she died, she left an extraordinary will. She didn't have much in the way of possessions, so she drew up a list of principles to pass on which concluded with the statement, "Faith, courage, brotherhood, dignity, ambition, responsibility—we must cultivate them and use them as tools for our task of completing the establishment of equality for the Negro . . . The Freedom Gates are half ajar. We must pry them fully open . . . I pray now that my philosophy may be helpful to those who share my vision of a world of Peace."

> 66 You white folks have long been eating the white meat of the chicken. We Negroes are now ready for some of the white meat. 99
> —*Mary McLeod Bethune*

A Cotton Pickin' Shame

Eli Whitney is generally credited with the invention of the cotton gin which transformed the South; and his creation was recognized as the most important American invention up to that point. There was only one problem—it was the idea of thirty-seven-year-old Georgia plantation owner **Catherine Lidfield Greene,** widow of Revolutionary War hero General Nathanael Greene. Catherine not only thought of the idea and told Eli about it, but let him live in her house, supported him while he perfected it, and helped make modifications to it for him. But when it came time to register it, ungrateful Eli applied for a patent under his name only and ended up with all the glory.

8.

Rulebreakers

and

Renegades

$\mathscr{S}$outhern women have always been strong and gone their own way. And that has led to some pretty amazing accomplishments indeed, as you will discover. African American women in particular, slaves and descendants of slaves, just didn't have as much to lose from not playing by the rules. But they were joined by some pretty sassy white sisters too!

Go Down, Moses

*T*he bravest and most daring conductor on the Underground Railroad, **Harriet Tubman's** heroic exploits included an estimated nineteen trips into the South, during which she led over 200 slaves to freedom. She became such a threat to southern slave owners that they offered a $40,000 reward for her capture, dead or alive. In addition, she earned distinction during the Civil War as the only woman in American military history to plan and execute an attack on enemy forces.

Born around 1821 on a plantation on Maryland's east shore, her parents, descendants of the Ashanti, named her Araminta; and, as a child, she was known as "Minty." As she grew older, she took her mother's name, Harriet. She worked as a field hand, which enabled her to develop enormous physical strength and endurance. At the young age of thirteen, she demonstrated that she was willing to put her life on the line for the cause of emancipation when she intervened to protect another slave from an overseer. Her reward was a near-fatal head wound that left her with a life-long affliction; and she suffered recurring seizures. The wound also left a horrific scar, a testament to the violence of the blow; and, from then on, she always kept her head covered.

As a teenager, Harriet had a vision of the Mason-Dixon Line and the fertile fields of opportunity blooming to the north in a dream. "Beautiful white ladies stretched out their arms to me over the line," she recalled. But their imaginary efforts were of no use. Her greatest fear was that her owner might die, and that she would be sold into the deep South, and that her family would be dispersed. In her late twenties, she learned her fear was soon to become reality. As she planned her escape, her husband, John Tubman, not only refused to go but threatened to tell of her plan. Harriet did manage to escape; and, when she returned for him months later, he had taken another wife.

After making her way north, Harriet found work in Philadelphia as a domestic. There she made the contacts she needed to return to Maryland to rescue her sister. This was the first of her legendary missions as an agent of the Underground Railroad. On these trips she used a variety of different disguises, alternately appearing as a hideous, crazy street person, or perhaps as an insane, old woman chasing chickens down the road. Hiding in the woods or fields outside of plantations, she would signal her presence through the singing of hymns. Several spirituals are attributed to Harriet Tubman, including "Wade in the Water." She always carried a pistol to dissuade any of her frightened fugitives from abandoning ship. "You'll be free or die," she told them, and she never once lost a passenger. Her courage and faith on these long journeys was so com-

pelling, she came to be called Moses, for leading her people to the promised land; other times she was known as General Tubman.

Harriet, in addition to her daring raids, was a prominent member of the abolitionist movement, giving speeches and personal testimony. She even conspired with John Brown on his raid of the federal arsenal at Harper's Ferry, although illness prevented her from taking part. When the Civil War broke out, she threw herself into battle, serving as spy, scout, and nurse for the Union Army. It was in June of 1863 that she led a Union raid, which resulted in the freeing of 750 slaves. She was at many of the great Civil War battles, including the Battle of Fort Wagner, which is celebrated in the 1990 film, *Glory*. There she served the last meal to Colonel Robert Gould Shaw of the Black Massachusetts Fifty-Fourth Regiment.

Her final home was in Auburn, New York, in a house that had acted as a way station for the Underground Railroad. In 1896, she purchased the twenty-five acres adjoining the house and built The Harriet Tubman House for Aged and Indigent Colored People, now a national landmark. She died in 1913.

66 There was one of two things I had a right to, liberty, or death; if I could not have one, I would have the other; for no man should take me alive. 99
—Harriet Tubman

BRAINY BELLE

It was 1804 and no decent Southern lady went to college; for finishing schools were the appropriate way to usher a proper belle into society. But **Barbara Blount Hall** wanted to sink her teeth into a real education, and, in the true belle spirit, registered to study philosophy at the University of Tennessee. Interestingly enough, the school let her in, even though universities wouldn't formally accept women until the 1890s. But in a chauvinistic move, Barb wasn't allowed standard grading for her courses like her male counterparts. Assumed to be too unladylike a system for the brainy belle, Barbara received comments such as "diligent." Her diligence, however, slammed open the doors of academia and taught foolish men that to assume anything merely makes an A-S-S out of U and M-E.

Up, Up, and Away

*F*earless **Tiny Broadwick,** born Georgia Ann Thompson in Granville County, North Carolina, was not one for staying in one place. She was the first person in the world to make a parachute jump from a hydroplane and one of the first people to do it from a airplane. (Tiny thought there had been a man who jumped before her, so being the modest type, was willing to accede the number one spot.) And during her lifetime, the feisty free-flyer made about one thousand parachute jumps from balloons, beginning in 1908.

Such adventures were not without hazards, however. Places she landed included treetops, telephone wires, on the roof of buildings, and in rivers and streams. Once she even missed the back of a horse by just two feet! "Another time," she recalled in the December 1, 1945, issue of *The State, A Weekly Survey of North Carolina,* "I saw a railroad train underneath me. A rather strong wind was blowing and it was difficult to regulate the course of the parachute even to the slightest degree. The engineer saw me. He realized what was

happening, so he put on his brakes. I hit the rear end of the train just as it was coming to a stop. My right elbow went through a coach window, but I wasn't cut very much." Humble Tiny was one lucky lady. The injury count on her eleven years of free-falling from the sky included one broken arm, a slightly fractured back, and two or three ankle sprains.

The diminutive dame—she weighed less than one hundred pounds—first became interested in her future profession when she attended a carnival in Durham in 1908 and saw Charles Broadwick, billed as "The Famous French Aerialist," parachute out of a balloon. Adrenaline coursing through her body, her first sky dive was just two days later! Explaining the result of that dive, Tiny understated many years later, "At that time I didn't know how to regulate the course of a parachute; otherwise there would have been no necessity for me to have landed in the bush." Eventually, Charles adopted Tiny as his daughter; and they toured the country, drawing crowds at county fairs and carnivals.

But, with the Wright Brothers historic flight in 1903, the world was ushered toward a new way of air travel, one that Tiny would eventually conquer through her aerial acrobatics. In 1913, she hooked up with Glenn Martin, an aviator who was displaying his plane at Griffith Park in Los Angeles. Always the clever businesswoman, Tiny explained that he would draw much larger crowds if he could announce a woman was going to jump from a plane and volunteered herself—for the bargain price of $500. (That would become her going rate. By the end of her career, her going rate had dropped to $300, presumably because too many other people were doing the same tricks.) Soon after her famous leaps from airplanes began, Tricky Tiny was selected by the government to demonstrate the safety of parachutes and subsequently equipped all of its planes with parachutes.

It was hard for Tiny to stop jumping. She retired for four years after getting married in 1916, then went back to it again in 1920. It was in her blood and the tenacious brave belle took to the skies again. She retired for good in 1922, but, as late as 1945, admitted to missing it.

BARRIER BUSTER

Georgian **Jacqueline Cochran Odlum** took to the skies in 1932. It was a long way up for a woman who called herself "a refugee from Sawdust Road—she never knew her parents and never owned a pair of shoes until she was eight years old," according to *Georgia Women: A Celebration*. From the 1930s through the 1950s, jaunty Jackie set and broke many airplane and jet records: the world's outstanding woman aviator three years in a row, the first woman to fly a bomber across the Atlantic, the only civilian ever to win the Distinguished Service Medal, and the first woman to crack the sound barrier and probably a few heads along the way.

COMMIE BELLE

*W*hile the South is generally known as a bastion of conservative politics, the region also gave birth to one of the most prominent American Communists in recent history, **Angela Davis,** who remains one of the most controversial people in the United States today. An active member of the Communist Party, the Black Panthers, and the Student Nonviolent Coordinating Committee, she succeeded in making enemies out of the most powerful people in government, including former Governor of California, Ronald Reagan. Her name became a household word in 1970 when she was placed on the FBI's ten-most-wanted list on charges of murder, conspiracy, and kidnaping, crimes that she did not commit.

Born in 1944, the future radical agitator grew up in a middle-class family in Birmingham, Alabama. Her mother was a schoolteacher; and her father owned a gas station. Both her mother and grandmother were political activists and worked to instill a deep sense of outrage in the young Angela over the condition of African Americans in the South. While still in elementary school, she was participating in the civil rights marches that were beginning to erupt in the 1950s.

A brilliant and committed student, she earned entrance to a progressive high school in New York and then to Brandeis University, where she studied philosophy with Herbert Marcuse, who deeply affected her ideas of social responsibility. While attending Brandeis, four girls that Angela had known were killed in Birmingham in 1963, when a church was bombed. Outraged by the violence, her radicalism began to develop deeply personal roots.

She spent her junior year abroad studying at the Sorbonne in France, where she became involved with Algerian students who were struggling against French colonialism. She returned to Europe after graduating from Brandeis, to study philosophy in Frankfurt at Goethe University. While there she again became deeply involved in a radical socialist student group demonstrating against the Vietnam War.

By 1967, she resolved to return to the United States to again study with Herbert Marcuse, who was now teaching at the University of California at San Diego. While working toward her doctorate, she became involved in the struggle for civil rights, and,

in 1969, convinced that revolutionary socialism was the only hope for black Americans, joined the American Communist Party and became involved in the Black Panthers. Also in 1969, she was hired to teach philosophy at the University of California at Los Angeles and became a popular teacher, but when her membership in the Communist Party was revealed, the Board of Regents and then Governor Ronald Reagan fired her. She sued to get her job back and won, but that wasn't the end of her problems, by any means. From then on her classes were closely monitored, and she began to receive death threats. Fearing for her life, she purchased several guns and had them legally registered.

In August 1970, Jonathon Jackson took these guns from Angela's house and hijacked

the Marin County Courthouse in retaliation for the murder, by guards at Soledad Prison, of his brother (also a close friend of Angela's), Black Panther George Jackson. In the aftermath, a judge, two prisoners, and Jonathon Jackson himself, were dead. Not waiting around to be served with a warrant, Angela went on the lam; and the middle-class philosophy professor was placed on the FBI's ten-most-wanted list. She was arrested two months later in New York and was imprisoned for almost two years await-ing trial. A nationwide "Free Angela" campaign soon erupted. Singer Aretha Franklin was motivated to post Angela's bail, "not because I believe in communism, but because she's a Black woman who wants freedom for all Black people." Released on $102,000 bail in February of 1972, she was subsequently acquitted of all charges.

All was not forgiven however, and Ronald Reagan and the regents took the extraor-dinary step of voting that Angela never be allowed to teach at a state-supported school in California. Despite this excommunication, she never apologized for her politics, and continues to offend and harass the powers-that-be in her strident campaign for equal rights. She ran for Vice President in 1980 and again in 1984 on the Communist Party ticket. Her career in academia also continues, as she has lectured and taught at various colleges in California. In the early 1990s, despite Ronald Reagan's resolution, Angela Davis, never one to compromise her beliefs and values, began teaching philosophy at the University of California at Santa Cruz, encouraging the defense of civil rights and deeply motivated by her firm roots stretching deep into southern soil.

The Cleopatra of Georgia

It was the spring of 1540 and Spanish explorer Hernando De Soto and his men were wandering around the area surrounding the Savannah River, not far from where Augusta, Georgia, is today. While there, they came upon a band of Native Americans afloat on the river. In one decorated and roofed canoe, a very large woman was enthroned, being drawn across the river by a second canoe that held her warriors. One of the astonished Spaniards compared her to Cleopatra on the Nile. Not speaking the language, De Soto dubbed her **"Queen of the Corachiqui"** and gave her a ruby and gold ring. In return, she presented him with a necklace of pearls long enough to wrap around her neck three times and still touch her knees. This gesture excited the greedy Spaniards, who became convinced she could lead them to a vast array of treasures. Fearful of the Spaniards' wrath, the queen gave them access to her tribe's burial grounds, where hundreds of pounds of river pearls were stored.

However, this wasn't enough for the greedy conquistadors. When they had taken enough and decided to depart, they forced the queen to come with them for they were convinced she could show them even more great riches. But the forceful queen of the wild was not about to take being kidnapped without a fight. After a few days, she managed to escape during the night, taking the trunk of pearls with her. History doesn't tell us what De Soto had to say when he found out that the clever woman had absconded with his ill-gotten gains; but it has shown us that the quickest way to a woman's heart is through jewelry, and, to her wrath, is the lack of it.

First Lady of Civil Rights

"*My* only concern was to get home after a hard day's work," said **Rosa Parks,** in response to questions about why she refused to give up her seat on a segregated Montgomery bus ride on December 1, 1955, an act that mobilized the Civil Rights movement of the 1950s. Truth is, however, that the Alabama native, once dubbed the "most mannerly rebel," had always had a strong consciousness of the problems of segregation in the South.

Born in 1913 in Tuskegee, Alabama, she learned about the hardships of slavery from her maternal grandparents and her experience in segregated schools made her realize discrimination was wrong. In 1943, she joined the Montgomery NAACP, one of the first women to do so. Working as an insurance salesperson, an office clerk, and a seamstress to help supplement her husband Raymond's income as a barber, she was also a member of the Montgomery Voters League, urging blacks to register to vote. Whenever she could, she "avoided the segregated drinking fountains, the 'Colored Only' elevators, and other reminders of the low status imposed on blacks in the South," notes *Epic Lives: One Hundred Black Women Who Made a Difference.* "She often walked home from work." Just before the famous incident when she refused to give up her seat, she had completed a summer civil rights seminar at the Highlander Folk School in Grundy County, Tennessee.

Following her jailing, she and her husband both lost their jobs (ultimately leaving town and moving to Detroit in 1957) and received threatening phone calls as the bus boycott heated up. She spoke often in support of the boycott, which also brought young minister Martin Luther King, Jr. to prominence. Finally after a year, the courts ruled that segregation on city buses was illegal. However, the struggle for civil rights throughout the United States was only just beginning.

Considered the "Mother of the Freedom Movement," Rosa Parks is the recipient of many awards including the Martin Luther King, Jr. Nonviolent Peace Prize and the Eleanor Roosevelt Woman of Courage Award. She has a street named after her in Detroit; and the Southern Christian Leadership Conference has given an annual award in her name since 1963. In 1987, she established the Rosa and Raymond Parks Institute for Self-Development, which works with young people, between the ages of eleven and fifteen, teaching tolerance and sensitivity. The simple act of saying "no" made this quiet rebel's serious intentions a "shout" heard round the world.

BOYCOTTING BELLE

Rosa Parks' action was the match, but the flames of freedom were fanned largely due to the efforts of renegade Southerner, **Jo Ann Robinson.** In 1955, Jo Ann was serving as the head of the Local Woman's Political Council in Montgomery, Alabama, when she learned that Rosa had been jailed. A professor at Alabama State College, she saw it as a chance to put into action a long-conceived plan of a city-wide bus boycott. She and two students clandestinely used the college's mimeographing equipment to print out over 50,000 flyers calling for the boycott. By morning, these motivated belles were peppering the city; and history was in the making.

SISTERS ARE DOING IT FOR THEMSELVES

*N*ot every Southern white woman in the 1800s was in support of slavery. Two of the South's most famous abolitionists were sisters **Sarah and Angelina Grimke,** who grew up as two of twelve children among the southern gentility of their father's plantation in Charleston, South Carolina. While other girls were thinking of their first cotillions and deb balls, Sarah and Angelina were concerned and outraged by the cruelty of slavery. The rebellious duo first encountered trouble in 1804, when Sarah, age twelve, taught a slave child how to read and write. A criminal offense during slavery—black illiteracy was thought to keep slaves more docile and compliant—Sarah bullishly and belle-ishly did it purposefully. Because Angelina supported her action, both were punished.

In 1830, the two sisters moved North, became Quakers, and took active roles in both abolition and women's suffrage. Each woman was a powerful orator in her own way, enduring a great deal of castigation from people who believed that women simply should not speak in public. In 1837, the Ministerial Association of Massachusetts issued a letter accusing them of behavior unbecoming to women; but, the church be damned—the sisters continued to speak out, demanding to be heard and not taking no for an answer.

They each wrote a number of abolitionist pamphlets, including Angelina's famous "Appeal to the Christian Women of the South." "I know that you do not make the laws, but I also know you are wives and mothers, the sisters and daughters of those who do," she wrote. Designed to be read by Southern women, it was more well known in the North, because Southern postmasters would destroy copies as they were mailed, warning the sisters never to return to the South.

In 1838 in Philadelphia, Angelina married a noted abolitionist minister, Theodore

Weld, in front of an integrated group of their friends, instigating outrage throughout Pennsylvania. (There was no word recorded, however, on what society thought, when several years later, Sarah married a black man.) Later, Angelina gave a passionate speech at an abolitionist convention in Philadelphia, which set off riots resulting in the tragic burning of the Shelter for Colored Orphans.

As pious Quakers, this turn of violence shook the sisters deeply, thereafter limiting their public speaking appearances. Also, as time went on, Sarah was more and more taken with the issue of women's rights, lamenting to a friend in 1852 about her lack of educational opportunities. "Had I received the education I craved and been bred to the profession of law, I might have been a useful member of society, and instead of myself and my property being taken care of, I might have been a protector of the helpless." Many years ahead of their time, the trail blazing Grimkes cleared some of the very first pathways for future generations of women and people of color throughout the nation.

66 The one doctrine of my mother's teaching which was branded upon my senses was that I should never let anyone abuse me. 'I'll kill you, gal, if you don't stand up for yourself,' she would say. 'Fight and if you can't fight, kick; if you can't kick, then bite.' 99
    — *Cornelia, born into slavery in Tennessee, in 1844*

MAKING A DIFFERENCE

White Southerner **Jessie Daniel Ames** had her own response to racism. She first turned her attention to women's rights and was largely responsible for Texas being the first southern state to ratify the female vote-giving Nineteenth Amendment, and founded the Texas League of Women Voters in 1919. Early on, she focused her attention on the large number of lynchings of black men in the name of "protecting 'virtuous Southern womanhood,'" notes *The Book of Women*. In the '30s, she moved to Atlanta and founded the Association of Southern Women for the Prevention of Lynching, targeting the wives and mothers of white male southerners most likely to engage in lynching, and educating whites to the truth that fewer than one-third of all lynchings happened because of rape or even its accusation. She exposed the racism at the roots of such violence and incurred the wrath of many residents. Women's groups began to support her cause, however; and, in 1940, there were no known or reported lynching cases in the South. The group disbanded in 1941. Jessie Ames broke ground as a teacher of tolerance; however, the heinous and illegal practice of lynching continues today in some areas of the country.

THE PEN IS MIGHTIER THAN THE SWORD

*T*hrough the violence, turmoil, and activism of the post-antebellum South, the pen of **Ida B. Wells** left an indelible mark on American history. An ardent advocate of civil, economic, and women's rights, her fearless devotion to justice often placed her in physical danger; but personal tragedy, threats of violence, or economic deprivation would not deflect her from her pursuit of truth.

Born to slaves in Holly Springs, Mississippi, in 1862, she was the eldest of eight children. Her parents believed strongly in education; and, after emancipation, they sent their children to school as early as possible. While Ida was attending high school at the age of sixteen, a yellow fever epidemic swept through Holly Springs; and both of her parents and one sibling were among the victims. Another brother had died several years earlier of spinal meningitis. The responsible sixteen-year-old Ida then assumed the care for her five remaining siblings. Pretending to be eighteen, she passed the teacher's exam and landed a teaching position at a school five miles from home at the monthly salary of $25. A year later, at the invitation of her mother's sister, she moved to Memphis, Tennessee, where she secured a better teaching job at a higher salary.

In May 1884, Ida boarded a train and sat down in the ladies' coach. The conductor demanded that she move to the segregated car. She describes what ensued after she refused to move, "He tried to drag me out of the seat, but the moment he caught hold of my arm I fastened my teeth in the back of his hand." The conductor had to enlist the help of two other men before they finally succeeded in dragging her from the train. She sued the company, and although she won an initial settlement of $900, the ruling was later appallingly overturned by the United States Supreme Court.

A prolific reader and debater, Ida began writing for two weekly newspapers that were key sources of communication in the black community at that time. Published under the pen name Iola, her popular weekly columns reached mostly rural, uneducated people. In 1889, she bought a one-third interest in Memphis' *Free Speech and Headlight*, later becoming its editor. Many of her articles were dedicated to the poor conditions of local schools for African American children. As a result, the white school board did not renew her teaching contract; and she was forced to earn an income by selling subscriptions to the *Free Speech*.

In May 1892, three close friends of Ida's, who were successful managers of a grocery store just outside Memphis, were accused of conspiracy and lynched. It was widely thought in America at that time that lynchings generally happened to blacks accused of rape. Ida began to investigate cases of lynching and discovered that, contrary to popular belief, lynchings happened primarily to financially independent black Americans. She published her findings, and, in addition, wrote a scathing editorial suggesting that white women were often attracted to black men. Fortunately, when the editorial appeared, Ida was en route to Philadelphia. The offices of the *Free Speech* were destroyed by an angry mob, and threats were made against her life. She did not return to the South for the next 30 years, moving to New York and getting a job at *The New York Age*, where she continued to raise hell.

Ida married Ferdinand Barnett, owner of the *Chicago Conservator*, in 1895, and moved to Chicago where she raised four children. Her husband was her most ardent supporter and encouraged her to continue her anti-lynching and political activities. She became such a prominent figure that she was one of only two African American women to sign the call for the formation of the National Association for the Advancement of Colored People in 1909. She later broke with the organization because she felt they were too timid.

It was also around 1910, that she began to write articles arguing forcefully that the vote was the key to economic, social, and political equality for African Americans. In 1913, she organized the Alpha Suffrage Club, the first African American female suffrage club in Illinois. Also in 1913, she attended the National American Womens' Suffrage Association's parade in Washington, D.C., where white Illinois delegates pleaded with her to march in back with the black delegates; but she refused. Through the sheer force of her personality as well as a great deal of perseverance, she successfully integrated the suffrage movement in the United States.

Ida believed strongly that agitation, activism, and protest were the only means of change in the U.S. She became increasingly at odds with other black leaders like Booker T. Washington, whom she saw as an accommodationist, and often spoke in support of Marcus Garvey and W. E. B. DuBois. As a result, the U.S. Secret Service labeled her a dangerous radical. Despite this, she continued to write, campaign, speak, and agitate in the name of equality, justice, and peace. She died in Chicago in 1931.

I SAID, I DON'T DO WINDOWS

Dorothy Lee Bolden took her first job in 1930, at the age of seven, washing diapers after school for $1.25 a week. Five years later, she got a raise when she took a job cleaning house for $1.50 a week. In 1968, Dorothy used her decades of experience as a domestic to found the National Domestic Workers Union in Atlanta. The group succeeded in forcing higher wages and better working conditions for their members and became an ongoing model for domestic workers in other cities nationwide.

INDOMITABLE SPIRIT

*W*ho in the United States doesn't know the story of **Helen Keller**? Born June 27, 1880, in Tuscumbia, Alabama, she was left blind, deaf, and mute at the age of nineteen months, as a result of a childhood illness. She grew up a spoiled, destructive, and increasingly uncontrollable child, locked in her own world, unable to communicate with society. No one who knew her would have believed that this indomitable spirit

would become one of the most famous, inspiring, and charismatic women the South has ever produced.

Through the Perkins Institute in Boston, Helen's parents hired the formerly blind Anne Sullivan (Macy), then twenty, to be Helen's teacher and governess. Anne arrived in Alabama in March of 1887, and, after two weeks of nonstop effort, was able to make contact with Helen, in an episode that has since become legendary, by placing her hands under a water pump and using sign language to spell "water" into them. Helen later said, "I knew then that 'w-a-t-e-r' meant the wonderful cool something that was flowing over my hand. That living word awakened my soul, gave it light, hope, joy, set it free!" In a few months, Helen learned the entire alphabet, over 300 words, and by mid-July had written a letter to her mother.

In 1888, Helen and "Teacher," as Helen called Sullivan, moved to Boston so that Helen could become a regular student at the Perkins Institute, where she studied for six years. In 1894, they moved to New York to the Wright-Humason School, established to teach oral language to deaf children. Their expenses were underwritten by John Spaulding, a sugar millionaire. However, Helen's speech did not improve and would always be unintelligible to all but her closest friends. She did, however, learn to read lips with her fingers and conquered New York society, meeting some of the most prominent people of the day, including writers Mark Twain and William Dean Howells.

Despite her physical challenges, Helen's love of learning was insatiable; and, with her brilliant and intuitive teacher, she was able to achieve what so many viewed as impossible. In 1890, she passed the entrance exams and gained admission to Radcliffe College. There she took a full course load and was accompanied to every class by Anne, who spelled each lecture into her hands. Helen's writing came to the attention of the editors at the *Ladies' Home Journal*, who persuaded her, while still at Radcliffe, to write her autobiography. With the help of a young Harvard University literature instructor, John Albert Macy, she wrote and published *The Story of My Life* in 1902. The book became an instant classic. In June 1904, Helen graduated cum laude from Radcliffe with the additional citation, "excellent in English letters," a previously unthinkable achievement for a deaf, dumb, and blind person.

After college, Helen and Annie moved to Wrentha, where Helen continued to write. In order to earn an income, the duo began to tour the country lecturing. At this point in her life, Helen also began to get involved in politics. Already a militant suffragist, in 1909 she became a member of the Socialist Party. A red flag hung in her study; and socialism gave direction and meaning to her writing and work. She published a collection of socialist essays in 1913, entitled *Out of the Dark*. Her controversial political stances included passionate opposition to World War I, the abolition of child labor, opposition to capitol punishment, and support of Margaret Sanger's birth control movement. In addition, her public support of the NAACP enraged her Alabama relatives; and she was increasingly subject to public attack as a result of her beliefs.

From the mid-1920s on, she would help to raise money for the American Foundation for the Blind, as well as promote legislation for the blind. With Helen's help, this organization quickly came to the attention of the public and accomplished numerous gains on behalf of handicapped Americans.

Continuing to write, tour, lecture and advocate, Helen achieved international fame on a level that few others have attained. Her travels took her through Europe, Australia, New Zealand, Latin America, the Middle East, and South Africa. At the invitation of the Japanese blind, she toured Japan twice, once in 1938 and again in 1948, where she pledged to fight against the horrors of atomic war. During World War II, she threw herself into the war effort, finding her niche in morale-building tours of military hospitals.

A Southern belle who chose to free herself from silence and darkness, Helen Keller overcame seemingly insurmountable handicaps to leave her mark on history as a writer, feminist activist, advocate for the disabled, and undeniable charismatic presence. As President Kennedy told her, several years before her death in 1968, "You are one of that select company of men and women whose achievements have become legendary in their own time."

❝ One can never consent to creep when one feels an impulse to soar. **❞**
   —Helen Keller

Five With Southern Moxie

Something Different

Rita Reutter was a fifty-eight-year-old grandmother of fourteen and graduate student at Florida Technological University in Orlando, when she decided to run for 1976 Homecoming Queen. Her campaign motto: "You can have a cutie pie any time. Let's have something different." She won.

Belle in a Barrel

Forty-three-year old **Anna Edson Taylor** owned a Texas ranch; and, as you might guess, that can be mighty expensive. So in 1901, she decided to take a dare and became the first person to go over Niagara's Horseshoe Falls in a (cushioned) barrel. After plummeting the famous 167 feet, she suffered only shock and a few cuts; and she won enough money to pay an installment on her ranch loan.

Road Rambo

In 1910, **Regina Rambo** (really!) **Benson** became the first woman to drive a car around the state of Georgia as part of a contest to promote Georgia's roads. She won a silver cup and the title "Expert Autoist." The 900-mile trip was not without its costs, however. She got a ticket for going over the twelve-mile-per-hour limit and her car had to be pulled from a creek. Regina, always a rulebreaker, ran for Congress on an anti-Prohibition ticket, in 1932. She lost.

JUMPING THE GUN

Mary Jarett White couldn't wait to vote. The Nineteenth Amendment gave women the right to vote as of August 1920. But this Georgian native actually voted in her state's spring 1920 election and had been on the roster as a registered voter since 1919. Just how she did it no one seems to know.

COMANCHE BELLE

Cynthia Parker was nine years old when Comanche warriors attacked Fort Parker in the Texas Territory in 1836, killing her family and carrying her off as one of their own. She lived happily with the tribe for the next twenty-four years, until she was kidnaped against her will by the Texas Rangers. In the meantime, she married the great Comanche chief Nacona and had two children, one of whom, Quanah Parker, became the greatest chief in Comanche history.

"Let It Shine"

*F*annie Lou Hamer was a middle-aged Ruleville, Mississippi, sharecropper when she responded to the Student Non-Violent Coordinating Committee's 1962 call to southern blacks to register to vote. The "short, squat, plain woman," as she described herself, who had a limp from polio, went with seventeen other would-be voters to the courthouse to register. Sheriffs and state troopers ringed the building and the group hesitated, until Fannie Lou marched off the bus and into history. She failed to pass the rigged test, as did her companions; and, when news of her attempt leaked out, she and her husband were booted out of the plantation land on which they had lived and farmed for over eighteen years. The water department even tried to bill them $9,000 in back bills for a home that had no running water!

Like any smart belle, Fannie Lou got mad and chose to get even; so she made another visit to the courthouse and succeeded in registering by convincing officials that she would keep coming back, every day if necessary, until she passed the test. One of twenty children of sharecroppers, she had seen first hand the workings of racism. When her father, after years of scrimping and saving, had enough money to buy two mules, whites poisoned the beasts to teach him a lesson about staying in his "place." That insult and the action at the courthouse politicized Fannie Lou, who went on to become a staunch civil rights activist.

In 1963, she was arrested coming home from a meeting—she and her friends decided to eat in a whites-only section of a bus terminal—and was beaten bloody while in jail. A jailer said to her, "We're going to make you wish you were dead." Some of the damage was permanent—she became blind in one eye and her kidneys were seriously damaged from the blows.

"That which harms us only makes us stronger,"and Fannie Lou didn't let that stop her. In 1964, she ran for Congress, but all the votes cast for her were somehow disqualified. She vaulted into national prominence that same year as one of the leaders of the Mississippi Freedom Democrats, who attempted to unseat the all-white delegation to the Atlantic City Democratic National Convention on the basis that they had not been fairly elected since African Americans were not allowed to vote. By 1968, Fannie Lou's work finally paid off with passage of the Voting Rights Act and new rules that forced political parties to increase political participation by those who had been excluded.

Her activism continued until her death from cancer in 1977. Her personal slogan and inspiration came from the spiritual, "This little light of mine, I'm gonna let it shine." She was the founder of Headstart in her community and the 700-acre Freedom Farm Cooperative, and in 1971, helped start the National Women's Political Caucus.

66 I'm sick and tired of being sick and tired. **99**
   —Fannie Lou Hamer

They Did it Their Way

Gutsy Belle

On February 3, 1956, **Autherine Juanita Lucy** became the first black student to be admitted to the University of Alabama. The graduate student attended classes for a few days, but was then suspended "for her own safety" after she was pelted with rotten eggs and made the target of murderous chants. By the end of February, courts ruled that she must be readmitted. "That girl sure has guts," exclaimed NAACP lawyer and later Supreme Court Justice Thurgood Marshall. But Autherine's victory was short-lived for the next day she was expelled for making libelous statements (she accused the university administration of inciting the mob). She was invited to attend several European universities, but declined, eventually finding work as a teacher. Finally in 1988, she was invited to re-enroll at the university again; and, in 1992, both she and her daughter received degrees.

Southern Surgeon

Georgia Patton Washington, born in Grundy County, Tennessee, in 1864, was not only the first woman to receive a medical degree from Meharry Medical College in Tennessee (the year was 1893), she was also the first black woman in Tennessee to be licensed to practice medicine. A surgeon, she soon sailed for Liberia as a medical missionary, but eventually relocated to Memphis due to poor health and set up a private practice, dying at age thirty-four.

Real Life Norma Rae

Sally Field won an Oscar for her 1979 portrayal of a union organizer in *Norma Rae*. The woman on whom the movie was based is **Crystal Lee Sutton** of Roanoke Rapids, North Carolina. A millhand for J. P. Stephens, she led a successful union drive there in 1974 (the union had lost an election in 1958). But this time, with Crystal Lee's help, 1,685 of the 3,133 workers endorsed the union. At the time, textile jobs accounted for one out of four jobs in the southern states and 40 percent of all North Carolina jobs.

A Woman's Prerogative

Cicily Jordan was a widow woman in pre-revolutionary America and, due to the shortage of eligible females in the early days of the Virginia Colonies, widows were expected to remarry ASAP. But apparently hard-headed (and hard-hearted) Cicily had other plans; for when the Reverend Grevell Pooley proposed, she declared emphatically that she wasn't ready. Mistaking her vehement objections, the dumbfounded preacher took this as a pledge to marry him later and unfortunately cast about broadcasting that fact. Well, nothing raises a hellish belle's dander quicker than trying to be outdone by a man, much less an oafish one like Brother Pooley; and so Cicily, madder than a wet hen, quickly proposed and engaged her nuptial future to someone else. Ultimately, the poor minister sued her for breech of promise—and in a victory for all women caught short by the manipulations of a man—lost.

MARRIAGE MINDED MAGGIE

*M*argaret Lea was a seventeen-year-old belle from Perry County, Alabama, when she first took a trip to New Orleans to lay eyes on the rugged and raffish war hero, General Sam Houston. Smitten, she swore to meet him in person some day and three years later, at a garden party in Mobile, her wish came true. Solid Sam was flattered, felled by her affection, and soon proposed marriage. Anxious Margaret quickly agreed, but insisted that he first meet her prominent family. Sam, who had quite a reputation as a drinker and womanizer, was afraid of what the lovely lady's family would have to say about their proposed union. Finally, fearful of losing her affections, he relented and appeared on her doorstep. His fears were realized; for her family was horrified at the very prospect of a marriage. However, stubborn Maggie threw caution to the wind, ignored her family's warnings, and followed her heart, to become Sam's beloved bride (and subsequently the First Lady of Texas), until succumbing to yellow fever years later.

66 A woman has got to love a bad man once or twice in her life, to be thankful for a good one. **99**

—Margorie Kinnan Rawlings

Buccaneer Belle

In the early 1700s, the punishment for pirates was death by hanging. **Anne Bonny,** a captured sea-bound femme fatale, however, entered a plea of innocence (and pregnancy), thus escaping capital punishment. The daughter of a South Carolina attorney, she returned to the sea and eloped, to the Bahamas, with a sailor. Once there, the fickle dame left him for a privateer, Jack Rackam. Dressed as a man, she helped Jack steal a boat from the harbor. The two then gathered a pirate crew (of men and other boisterous belles bound for the sea) and plundered and pillaged the coast for the next several years. When their boat was captured in 1720, the crew was sent to Jamaica and sentenced to death by hanging. Two of the bloodthirsty pirates pleaded for clemency, and after a careful examination, the skeptical judges were startled to discover that they were indeed women, and pregnant! Anne Bonny and fellow pirateer Mary Read were thrown into prison and the rest of the crew hanged. Mary subsequently died in childbirth and Anne was eventually pardoned, but history has since lost track of the Pirate Princess and her babe.

9.

Murderous Madams and Other Bad Seeds

In general, the violent vixens immortalized here benefitted from the stereotype that women don't kill, maim, and torture. But obviously, belles do get even! That's why, for so many, the punishment didn't exactly fit the crime. Judges and juries just weren't convinced by, in the words of playwright Beth Henley's *Crimes of the Heart* belle-in-a-frenzy Babe McGrath—a good hearted daughter of Copiah County, Mississippi—who shot her husband and then offered him a glass of lemonade, explaining, "I was having a bad day."

NEVER CROSS A SOUTHERN BELLE

*T*he environs of Leland, Mississippi (population 5,000, just outside Greenville) are a dangerous place, at least for relatives of white, well-dressed, church-going females. It was here in 1966 that tea-drinking **Erma Abraham** killed her husband, a retired mail carrier, with a shot to the head from her .38. She arrived in designer suits for her trial, claimed her husband was impotent and forced her, according to an article by Julia Reed entitled "In Defense of Southern Womanhood," "into 'unnormal' sex acts, specifically cunnilingus. When that last word was printed in the [local] paper, it was, according to then-editor Hodding Carter III, for the first time." Besides, she claimed, she couldn't remember shooting him because she was suffering from "acute brain syndrome."

Erma got off scot free. Well, first she was found guilty by reason of insanity and was sentenced to the state mental hospital until "cured"—an incarceration and medical miracle in only two short months. She was later discovered to have embezzled tens of thousands of dollars from her employer, but was never actually tried, because the local prosecutor reasoned, "If she was crazy when she killed her husband, she must have been crazy when she took the money."

Leland is also the home of **Ruth Dickins,** who in 1948 chopped her seventy-year-old mother to pieces with hedge clippers, claiming "a negro" did it (bringing to mind the South Carolina murderess Susan Smith who recently drowned her children, also placing blame on a black man). Ruth "was from a fine old Delta family, had plenty of money, was married to a cotton broker and planter who was one of the most respected men around, and lived in a big, white house on the banks of Deer Creek with the rest of the Leland gentry" according to Julia Reed. She did get life imprisonment, but was also granted two ten-day holiday leaves to attend the presentation of her daughters at the

Delta Debutante Ball, and a three-month medical leave because she was allergic to the prison diet and had a "uterine disturbance" which caused "swimming of the head." Six years after her conviction, the governor commuted her sentence altogether—after all, anyone can have a bad day—and "she came back to take her place in the First Baptist Church, running the nursery school and teaching Sunday school," reports Reed. When she died in 1995, the obituary made no mention of the unsavory incident, focusing instead on her "'pioneer Delta heritage,' graduation from Hollins College in Roanoke, Virginia, her marriage, her extensive church involvement, and her membership in the Leland Garden Club."

BORN AGAIN VIRGIN

According to comedian **Florence King,** a renegade if there ever was one, the South is home to a bevy of "self-rejuvenating virgins," who, among other clever methods, rely on that "most southern of all contraceptives": a bottle of warm Coca-Cola, shaken and applied in the proper orifice.

Other Murderous Mrs.s

*E*xamples of leniency toward southern female criminals abound. In 1968, during a telecast of the Miss America pageant, **Peggy Bush** killed her lawyer husband after he yelled at their fourteen-year-old daughter about the bills she'd been running up at the country club. At her trial, she testified that he had been swearing at her—although she could not say the words, and used the initials g.d. and s.o.b instead—and that she thought the weapon was a "pop gun"—oops, it was a .22! In record time (three minutes, which still has not been broken), the jury declared her not guilty.

And who can forget **Becky Cotton** of Edgefield, South Carolina? In 1806, she was tried for the murder, by ax, of her third husband, and when authorities dredged the pond to find him, they also discovered the bodies of Becky's two previous husbands—one dead from poison and the other with a large needle stuck straight through his heart. An eyewitness account of her trial recalls: "as she stood at the bar in tears, with cheeks like rosebuds wet with morning dew and rolling her eyes of living sapphires, pleading for pity, their subtle glamour seized with ravishment the admiring bar—the stern features of justice were all relaxed, and judge and jury hanging forward from their seats, were heard to explain, 'Heavens! What a charming creature.'" Needless to say, she was found innocent and promptly married a jury member. Justice did prevail eventually—her brother murdered her.

THE TIE THAT BINDS

The Wardlaw sisters, Virginia, Caroline and Mary, were three daughters of a prominent Southern family at the turn of the 20th century who dressed all in black, didn't mingle with others, and moved frequently. The very picture of genteel southern grace, they supported themselves by teaching, and by killing relatives for their insurance money: Mary's son (by fire), Caroline's husband (from "undetermined causes"), and Caroline's daughter (drowned in the bathtub after being starved). When they tried to cash in the third policy (they had already collected $22,000), the plotting sisters were finally caught. Virginia starved herself to death in jail and Mary was acquitted. That left only Caroline, who was convicted, ruled insane, and relegated to a mental hospital.

❝No matter which sex I went to bed with, I never smoked on the street.❞
—*Florence King in* Confessions of a Failed Southern Lady

A BLAZING LOVE

$\mathscr{B}$orn during the Depression in the 1930s, Fannie Belle Fleming was a poor child of moonshiners living in a hollow up Twelve Pole Creek near Wilsondale, West Virginia. She and her ten brothers and sisters used to help her grandpappy make pot "likker" and hide out from the law. Cursed and blessed with a very large bust by the time she was thirteen, Fannie Belle attracted quite a bit of local male attention. But she wanted a better life for herself, so she hightailed it to Washington, D.C. at the age of sixteen, and eventually recreated herself as the famous stripper **Blaze Starr.**

She was good at what she did and began to get quite a reputation. But her career really took off after she moved to Baltimore and a writer for *Esquire*, in town to do an article about the city, featured her in the magazine. She began touring the country, always thinking up new, inventive acts and costumes. Once she experimented with a panther in her show, but had trouble with hotel personnel whenever she tried to check him in. Finally, when he took a swipe at her breast (her livelihood, as she said), she got rid of him. Working in Philadelphia, she became lovers with Frank Rizzo, then the police chief and later mayor, in order to try to get him to stop arresting her. Her scheme failed to work and eventually she relocated to New Orleans, where she met then Louisiana Governor Earl Long (and supposedly had a fling with John Kennedy, although she said nothing about that in her book).

In her autobiography, Blaze maintains that theirs was a true love match, that he had planned on divorcing his wife and marrying her, when he up and died. Previously, they had carried on a torrid (and notorious) affair; during their very public time together he showered her with gifts including a four-carat diamond, several mink coats, and other jewelry. When his wife got wind of his romance, Blaze contends, she had him institutionalized for insanity. He fought back, but the stigma cost him the next election and soon he died. She was bereft, but continued stripping, eventually buying a club and hiring many of her nieces and siblings to work for her.

In 1989, a movie was made based on her book, co-starring Paul Newman and Lolita Davidovich. In the movie, Earl asks Blaze, "Would you still love me as much if I wasn't the fine governor of the great state of Louisiana?" Upon which, she retorts, "Would you still love *me* if I had little tits and worked in a fish house?

66 I've learned one hell of a lot about men in my lifetime. They're all right to take to bed, but you sure better never let them get a stranglehold on you. **99**
   —*Blaze Starr*

Marvelous Southern Madams and Other Shady Ladies

- **Tempest Storm,** a well-known Georgia hooker with 40-21-34 measurements in the days before plastic enhancement, who wrote a book in her retirement.

- **Belle Brezing,** famed 19th century madame of a bordello in Lexington, Kentucky. As far as we know, she didn't write a book, but the character of Belle Watling in *Gone With the Wind* is supposedly modeled after her.

- **Josie Arlington,** an 1880s lady of the night from New Orleans who got into a cat fight over turf with Beulah Ripley. Beulah tore out most of Josie's hair. Josie retaliated by biting off a big hunk of Beulah's ear and a large portion of her lower lip. Josie's tomb in a Metairie cemetery boasts a statue of a young girl knocking at the tomb's entrance. Supposedly it is to symbolize that she never took virgins into her house of sin.

- **Emma Johnson,** also of New Orleans, was reputed to sell children of both genders into sex slavery and concocted a number of novel ways to make money from sadomasochism, fetishism, and voyeurism. From her home, she performed "lewd and abandoned" sex shows, as a newspaper in 1892 put it, when she was arrested and fined twenty dollars for failing to keep her blinds closed.

THE POETRY-WRITING GUN MOLL

In her time, **Bonnie Parker** was the most famous female outlaw in the world, which was somewhat surprising since she and partner Clyde Barrow were thieves of the most minor sort: They held up filling stations, Mom-and-Pop grocery stores, and tiny banks as they moved throughout the South (the most money they ever stole was $3,500). They did, however, manage to kill thirteen people in the process and elude police over and over again, while holding the rapt attention of the entire nation. Though her family described her as "a simple country girl who was deathly afraid of guns," police claim she herself killed at least three people and was an accomplice to at least six other murders.

Born in 1910 in rural Texas, Bonnie lost her father when she was four. Her mother then moved the family to Dallas where the intelligent, high-spirited child quickly grew into a feisty ninety-pound blonde ever eager for sex. She married her high school sweetheart Roy Thornton at sixteen, tattooing his name on her thigh (in general, tattooing for women didn't come into vogue until nearly seventy years later). Theirs was a stormy romance and Roy ended up in prison for murder in 1929. That's when Bonnie, "bored crapless" as she herself reported, met her destiny in the form of one Clyde Barrow.

The duo were an odd pair—a homosexual (him) and nymphomaniac (her), but somehow their relationship worked. It worked particularly well when they teamed up with Ray Hamilton, a cohort in crime who slept with both of them in an odd on-again, off-again love triangle. But Bonnie was loyal to Clyde in her way. When he was jailed for robbery, she slipped him a gun and distracted the guards so he could make an escape. Later however, when she was jailed briefly for robbery, he did not return the favor and subsequently she served the full three months. But the two were soon reunited and, teaming up with Clyde's brother, sister-in-law, and a former kidnap victim turned accomplice (after being ditched by Ray), began to rob and kill in earnest, garnering the full attention of the media and law enforcement.

The volatile gang's notoriety delighted Bad Bonnie. She began bombarding newspapers with samples of her poetry, including "The Story of Suicide Sal": "If he had returned to me sometime,/ though he hadn't a cent to give,/ I'd forget all this hell that he's caused me/ And love him as long as I live." And being a gal who knew how to have a good time, she also sent newspapers photos of herself "horsing around," smoking cigars, and brandishing a machine gun at Clyde, which, when published, only fanned the flames of their fevered celebrity.

In 1933, the gang shot its way out of a police trap in Joplin, Missouri, killing two cops. Soon after, as they were fleeing the scene of a crime, they had a fiery car crash and Bonnie received second and third degree burns over much of her body. She recovered, but knew their fateful end was near. In late 1933, she sent newspapers "The Ballad of Bonnie and Clyde," which ended: "Some day they will go down together/ And they will bury them side by side./To a few it means grief,/To the law it's relief/But it's death to Bonnie and Clyde," thus sealing the duo's stardom in the firmament of criminal infamy.

She was right too. On May 23, 1934, the police set another trap for them, this time in Gibland, Louisiana. Bonnie was eating a sandwich as the gunfire ripped through the air; she died as twenty-three bulletholes riddled her body.

BRILLIANT, TOUGH, AND COOL

Dorothy Faye Dunaway rocketed to international fame when the green-eyed epitome of the southern belle portrayed Bonnie Parker in the 1967 Arthur Penn movie, *Bonnie and Clyde*, a film that "marked the turn from western to southern settings in popular adventure dramas," according to *The Encyclopedia of Southern Culture.*

An "Army brat" and Bascom, Florida native, Faye Dunaway was nominated for an Academy Award for her performance. Her career flourished with roles in *Chinatown* (earning another nomination) and Paddy Chayefsky's brilliant *Network,* for which she won the Academy's Best Actress award in 1976. In

her long and luminous career, Dunaway is perhaps best remembered for her "all-hell's-broken-loose" portrayal of film legend Joan Crawford in *Mommy Dearest* (1981). In that role, the bellicose belle called upon her southern strength and iron will, bursting forward with the unforgettable declaration that became a mantra of the '80s, "No more wire hangers!" And who could forget the sight of Faye-as-Joan when she shrieked the immortal lines at a Pepsi Co. board-of-directors meeting after the death of her husband, "Don't f@%# with me fellas, it's not my first trip to the rodeo!!"

WHO DO VOODOO?

*W*hen you talk about southern "bad seeds," you can't ignore the voodoo queens. Voodoo queens were free women of color who presided over all voodoo rituals; this being a matriarchal world. While there are 50 million followers of voodoo worldwide, New Orleans was (and still is) the voodoo capital of the world in the mid 19th century when **Marie Laveau** and her eponymously named daughter reigned there. (True believers claim that there was simply one Marie, who was immortal.)

The first Marie was said to be "tall, handsome and mean-eyed," according to *New Orleans*, "the illegitimate daughter of a wealthy white planter and a mulatto." Married in 1815 at age nineteen, her husband mysteriously disappeared soon after. She took up hair-dressing, where she heard all the secrets of the white upper class, and began living with a man named Louis Christophe Duminy de Glapion, with whom she had fifteen children.

By 1830, she was the dominant voodoo force in the city—even the police and politi-cians were afraid of her—and is reputed to have eliminated all her rivals by voodooing them to death. "One of her bad-luck charms was supposedly a small bag made from the shoulder of a dead body. The contents included bats wings, cats eyes, a rooster's heart, and an owl's liver," reports *New Orleans*. It is claimed that her house contained two altars, one for good and the other for bad, as well as mummified babies and a very large snake. Most of her money and her power is said to have come from blackmail and by procuring attractive light-skinned black girls for wealthy white men. Marie died in 1881, but her daughter had already taken up the family profession, to equal terror and success. It is believed that the last Laveau practitioner died early in the 20th century (or did she?)

Some New Orleans voodoo women specialized in ministering to and against the pros-titutes in Storyville, the famous red light district that flourished in New Orleans in the mid-1800s. One was **Julia Jackson,** a six-foot-tall, cross-eyed woman who supposedly had a "sealing power" which could "close up a whore so she couldn't do no business," as reported in *Storyville, New Orleans*. She could also induce or terminate pregnancy and cause venereal disease from a distance. Rival ladies of the night would pay her to do in their enemies. Another such woman was **Lala,** who could make a prostitute so "hot" by putting red powder on one leg and green on the other, that she would have more business than she could handle. The most well-known was **Eulalie Echo,** who did only "good" voodoo such as seeing into the future, for example. She was the godmother of famed jazz musician Jelly Roll Morton, who, when he had trouble later in life, blamed it on his having been at Eulalie's seances.

Then there is **Minerva** of Beaufort County, South Carolina, immortalized in *Midnight in the Garden of Good and Evil*. "If I told you Minerva was a witch doctor or a voodoo priestess, I'd be close, "writes author John Berendt "She's that and more." In the book, he describes going to see her. "Minerva was sitting in a small room under a bare light bulb. She was like a sack of flour. Her cotton dress was stretched tight over her round body. Her skin was pale brown, and her face was as round as a tranquil moon. Her gray hair was pulled back in a bun except for two little pigtails, one hanging over each ear. She wore a pair of purple-tinted, wire-rimmed glasses. The table in front of her was piled high with bottles, vials, twigs, boxes, and odd bits of cloth. The floor was littered with shopping bags, some bulging, some empty. . . . Minerva put aside a small wax doll she'd been working on. 'It's after midnight now, . . . time for doin' evil.' . . . Minerva spoke unintelligible words in her dreamy, half-whispered voice. . . . use[ing] every prop she had brought with her—roots, charms, powders, squares of cloth. She put them on the ground in front of her and stirred them with two sticks as if mixing a voodoo salad."

TEMPER, TEMPER

Born in 1836, **Mary Jane Jackson** was a New Orleans prostitute by the age of thirteen. Nicknamed "Bricktop" for her flaming red hair, Mary Jane was known throughout the French Quarter for her fiery temper. A Poydras Street saloon owner took her as his live-in mistress, but she was soon back out on the street when an ensuing fight cost her former lover one ear and a big chunk of his nose. She eventually ended up at Archie Murphy's Dance Hall, a place where anything went. It was there in 1856 she committed her first murder, clubbing a man to death who called her a whore. The following year she killed a character called Long Charley, so named because he was seven-feet-tall and skeleton-thin. The charming pair started an argument over which way Charley would fall if she stabbed him to death, which was soon settled with one thrust of her custom-made two-bladed knife. (It was forward.)

Kicked out of Murphy's, she established her own house of ill repute with two other prostitutes. Eventually, she became embroiled in another barroom brawl, where a flash of the famous knife finally landed Mary Jane in jail for murder. (It took twelve policemen to contain her.) However, with the help of a well-placed bribe, the death was blamed on "heart trouble" and Bricktop was freed.

During her brief stint in jail, however, she had fallen in love with one of her jailers, John Miller, a convicted former killer with only one arm, who wore a ball and chain at the end of his stump. He quit his job and the pair launched a two-year love affair that featured more drunken brawls and outrageous scenes of public fornication. Marital bliss was not to last, however. One day Bricktop, once again wielding her trusted dagger, stabbed her man and went on the lam fleeing New Orleans, fearing yet another murder charge. Strangely enough, John Miller lived and begged her to return. She did so and upon her return was met by darling John with a bullwhip and a smile of pure evil. But ol' Bricktop proved stronger than he, wrestled the whip from him, ripped the ball and chain from his stub (well, he did try to brain her with it, after all) and killed him with her trusty knife.

This time the once crafty lass would not get off. Sentenced to ten years of hard labor, she served only nine months before Louisiana fell to Union troops during the war between the states and the military governor pardoned all felons. Never one to look a gift horse in the mouth, the outrageous Bricktop took the opportunity to quietly disappear and was never heard of again.

SHE DONE THE DECENT THING

Texan **Pearl Choate** was "a veritable Amazon, standing well over six-feet tall," reports *Bad Girls Do It!*, "tipping the scales at some 250 pounds in her prime." Born in 1907, she was a nurse who specialized in marrying men in their nineties with fat wallets, all of whom died shortly after the nuptials. By the 1950s, she had racked up six husbands. The only problem was that husband number six took four bullets to fell and so it was off to prison for Pearl, who served twelve years before being paroled for good behavior. In 1965, she married again and sure enough, the old millionaire soon expired. Authorities suspected Choate, but couldn't pin it on her. She told the press, "They keep bringing up my six other husbands. What's that got to do with today's love? They were all about Mr. Birch's age when I married them. So what? I done the decent thing. You never heard of Pearl Choate not marrying a man. Pearl Choate don't shack up."

TRIGGER HAPPY TEMPTRESS

*F*or **Laura Fair,** "a fluffy southern snowflake in the mid-1800s who drifted west trailing a string of dead-or-damaged husbands behind her," writes Autumn Stephens in *Wild Women,* "romance was a lot like target shooting. Practice, it seemed, made perfect — and in her opinion, it never hurt to pack a pistol. Let cute little Cupid claim his victims with arrows of tenderness: on the adults-only battlefield of love, chunks of hot lead constituted the *coup de grace* of choice.

"Then again, Fair's checkered background didn't precisely encourage the notion that love was any pastime for sissies. She first hit the great rifle range of matrimony at the impressionable age of sixteen; within a year, her spouse had perished under most mysterious circumstances. Husband Number Two skidded from the cooing-dove stage to the stupid-turkey stage in just six short months. 'He would shoot over the head of my bed, sir, with a pistol,' Fair testified at the divorce trial. 'Then he would go out and shoot the poultry in the yard, fifty at a time, one after another.' A better sport (and perhaps a better marksman), Husband Number Three left the birdshot alone, but blew himself out of the water when Fair made it clear she preferred to loll in some other guy's featherbed."

You would think that would be the end of love for the fluffy Fair. Nope, she then "gamely snapped up the proposal of Alexander Crittenden, a prominent San Francisco lawyer, six months after their starry-eyed meeting in 1863. Numerous cliches and misdemeanors, however, were to mar that ill-fated romance, starting with Alexander's startling confession that his wife did not understand him. Naturally, this revelation came as something of a shock to Laura, who had not previously realized her fiance was married. Nor did a three-way meeting of wife, mistress, and middleman result in the sort of amicable French arrangement Alexander had evidently hoped to broker. Not to worry, the adulterous attorney promised his ladylove, his marriage was a sham, and a divorce was definitely in the works.

"But after seven more years of sharing her still-married sweetheart with his spouse, fed-up Fair saw she'd have to take the separation into her own hands. 'You have ruined me!' she explained, and shot her procrastinating paramour through the heart."

Her trial was the sensation of the decade with witnesses for the prosecution supplying all kinds of juicy details about their amorous encounters with Laura. Reports Stephens, "A damsel so depraved as to enjoy a fulfilling sex life, it was implied, was doubtless guilty of far worse, and the trigger-happy temptress was sentenced to hang." However the sentencing was later overturned, when the Supreme Court decided she was guilty by reason of insanity (a southern lady's best defense).

66 To grow up female in the South is to inherit a set of directives that warp one for life, if they do not actually induce psychosis. 99
—*Shirley Abbott*

Rah! Rah! Rah! Sis Boom Bah!
My Mom Tried To Kill Your Mom!
Ha! Ha! Ha?

Among the most notorious recent Southern women killers, who can forget **Wanda Webb Holloway**, the Channelview, Texas housewife convicted in 1991 of murder for hire? She was just trying to be a good mother to her eighth-grade daughter, Shanna Harper, who was trying out for the school's cheerleading squad and was facing stiff competition in Amber Heath, a classmate who had gotten a spot on the squad two years in a row. Wanda had the bright idea that if she could have Amber's mother, Verna, "taken care of," the girl would be so grief-stricken that she would drop out of cheerleading, assuring her daughter of not only the plum cheerleading spot, but all the friends and dates that came with it.

So she hired and conspired with a hit man, actually her ex-brother-in-law, even giving him a pair of diamond earrings as a down payment. But the police got wind of the scheme before it could be carried out and it was off to the pokey for the so-called Cheerleader Mom. In 1991, she was tried and sentenced to fifteen years in prison and fined $10,000. But there was a snafu—a juror was later discovered to have been on probation and so Wanda's conviction was overturned. In 1996, as a second trial was about to take place, she plead no contest and received a ten-year sentence.

But like many other southern women before her, Wanda did not spend much time in prison. In February 1997, Judge George Godwin ruled that she would not benefit from any more prison time (she had served six months) and released her, under the condition that she perform 1,000 hours of community service as penance.

Hell's Belles

The cheerleading misadventures stirred up a whirlwind of tabloid fodder and at least two made-for-television movies, including HBO's *The Positively True Adventures of the Alleged Texas Cheerleader-Murdering Mom,* starring Holly Hunter as Wanda. And what ever happened to the battling junior belles? Back in 1991, with the murder plot foiled, both girls again tried out for the squad. Popular Amber made it for the third year in a row, while sinister Wanda's little Shanna was rejected, once again.

10

Tinkerbelles and Shrieking Violets

Southern lore and legend, and practically every branch of every solid family tree, has the proverbial misfit whom relatives refer to in whispered tones at family reunions, fearing exposure of that odd cousin, who stands just a little bit outside of the mainstream, often mired in controversy, and far removed from the conventional. There is, for example, Truman Capote's dotty and childlike, but ever-loveable, Aunt Sook made famous in his short story of growing up in rural Alabama, "A Christmas Memory." To some families of rigid manner and strong social standing, these figures proved somewhat of an embarrassment which at times led to the out and out rejection of the usually solitary figures. But the plethora of these strange relatives has continued to provide grist for the story mill of family folklore, spilling over with the color, humor, and quirkiness of these lovable (and often boisterous) characters and keeping the contemporary South firmly enmeshed in a world of neo-gothic mania and outrageousness.

The Queen of Tears and Mascara

In 1974, South Carolina televangelist Jim Bakker and his leaky fountain wife and cohort **Tammy Faye Bakker** (famous for her rivers of television tears of joy and sorrow which causes her copious trowel-applied makeup to run), founded the Praise the Lord (PTL) television ministry. PTL became a multi-million dollar empire before crashing and burning when it was revealed that former squeaky-turned-sneaky Jim had cheated on his wife with church secretary and future *Playboy* playmate Jessica Hahn and then used PTL-backed payola to try and cement her silence. Two silicone-enhanced breasts and an operation for a "deviated septum" pushed Jessica and the woe-begotten Christian couple into the media spotlight where they were trapped in a quagmire of scandal that rocked the religious right to its very core.

The ever valiant Tammy Faye tried to keep it together, though she was often seen wailing in public, literally "losing face." The Christian canary, known for her pop albums of contemporary gospel tunes, turned to her flock for support, but was eventually maligned along with her husband as the hanging thread pulled the entire tapestry apart.

Eventually they lost their big mansion with the solid-gold bathroom fixtures, expensive foreign cars and heated doghouse. Jim was sent to prison, in his own flood of tears, for selling 150,000 "lifetime partnerships" in the now-defunct ministry's Fort Mill, South Carolina Heritage USA theme park. (The partnerships were oversold, claimed prosecutors, with the Bakkers living off the ill-gotten gain.) The songbird soon got used to Jim's absence as he served his time in the pokey and Tammy's tears were soon dried as she divorced her husband of over thirty years to marry his best friend, Roe Messner, former chief builder at Heritage USA.

Life seemed to be back on track. She went from blonde to redhead ("it's a wig, honey," she giggled to reporters), and landed a new television show. A partnership with openly gay entertainer Jim J. Bullock, the new show emphasized entertainment, not salvation, and was called *The Jim J. and Tammy Faye Show*. She again sang, strutted, and tempted the fashion police as she giggled her way back before the viewing public. But she dropped her anchor seat after only six weeks. "The rigorous taping schedule and the stress that comes with a national television show is more than I can handle at this per-

sonally difficult time," she said in a written statement, although wags claim low ratings had more to do with her departure. What was her personal difficulty? Hubby number two was about to be imprisoned for federal bankruptcy fraud and Tammy, also dealing with the desire to avoid another public execution, was a mite bit upset.

The petite former evangelist with the "stretch-o-rama" smile, as the *Fort Worth Star-Telegram* once called it, said she was going to use her time to promote her new infomercial, but life had other plans for her. Only a month later, she was diagnosed with colon cancer and underwent chemotherapy, while Roe went to the pen. At the same time she developed other troubles of her own. In 1996, she and her former husband had dueling books published, each with their own version of the scandal that led to their downfall. Her book, *Tammy: Telling it My Way* paints Jessica Hahn as a "professional" temptress, and her ex as a poor slob who put too much trust in others and was goaded into having extramarital sex by a fellow preacher. In his version, he accepts more of the blame for the "Jessica" situation, but says he did it to make his wife jealous. She has a message for him in the book: "Jim, if you're reading this, here's my advice: Get on with your life and don't worry what people think. Hold your head up high." He, for his part, claims to still miss her.

What good came out of her being cast out of the garden of Eden? "I think an awful lot of people got their eyes opened and faced reality . . . and realized no one's perfect," says Tammy. "And in a way that's been good. It's caused people to look to God."

66 You don't have to be dowdy to be a Christian. **99**
— *Tammy Faye Bakker*

66 Did you hear what happened when they took off all of Tammy Faye's makeup? They found Jimmy Hoffa. **99**
— *joke floating about on the Internet*

"Your Sister's on the Corner Selling Nasty for Sale"

At six-feet-four-inches (give or take a few) tall in stocking feet, drag queen **RuPaul** Andre Charles is hard to miss. Raised in Atlanta, this gay firebrand has the sass of the most righteous southern belle. Favorite sayings include: "If I'm lying, I'm flying, and you don't see no wings, do ya?" "You can call me he, you can call me she, as long as you call me!" and "Don't let the smooth taste fool ya." When asked how tall he is, the Amazon-like entertainer replied, "with hair, heels, and attitude—through the roof!"

His 1995 autobiography *Lettin' It All Hang Out!* tells of his feeling different as a child; he used both male and female style influences since he was "just a little-bitty drag queen growing up in Georgia." Professionally, he got his start when he dressed as a woman for a mock wedding and decided he looked fabulous. He started going on an Atlanta community access television show called *The American Music Show,* then made his way to New York City, released three albums and several female personae including "Starbooty"—a cross between Emma Peel and "Get Christy Love,"—before hitting it big in 1992 with the song "Supermodel of the World" and an album of the same name from Tommy Boy Records. Inspired professionally by Diana Ross and personally by his mother, he has become a favorite of the video world, first appearing in the B-52s' "Love Shack" with an afro the size of a small planet. Dueting with such famous people as Elton John on his remake of "Don't Go Breaking My Heart," RuPaul has traveled the world entertaining and raising funds for AIDS charities. He has appeared in several movies including *The Brady Bunch Movie*(s), *Crooklyn,* and *To Wong Foo, Thanks for Everything, Julie Newmar.* Also appearing in many print advertisements for Baileys Irish Cream and NEC; he is a spokesperson, along with k.d. lang, for MAC Cosmetics, which he personally uses. (It takes him three hours to get in drag or "one hour fifteen

minutes in a pinch," reports his Atlanta-based fan club.) He is currently the host of his own self-named talk show on VH-1 Music Television, the host of the most popular radio show in New York City, and has recently released a new album entitled *Foxy Lady*.

From an ad for the video of *Starbooty*: "RuPaul is Starbooty . . . badder than Bond, more bullets than Rambo, sexier than Bo . . . six-feet-seven inches of raw power. She brought herself up from the ghetto to become one of America's top black models, and now she's an agent for the United States Government, fighting crime for the country that brought her up out of that mind thang. Get y'all alcohol off the streets, crack down on Crack, 'cause Starbooty's gonna kick some butt tonight."

Sporting Woolworth's Cameo pantyhose "because nothing beats a great pair of dimestore legs," shoes from Frederick's of Hollywood, and perfume "I recommend 'Whore'—for she who is," Ru lists the following as the drag queen's first three essentials: "Flawless, fierce attitude; disposable razors; shaving gel." His drag is a profession, according to his fan club. "When the lights are down and the paparazzi have gone home, Ru enjoys nothing more than sitting in his boxers with a remote in one hand."

66 The point of my whole image is really making fun of celebrities. It's making fun of this Madison Avenue concoction of what femininity is. You know, wigs and high heels have nothing to do with what a woman is. People ask, 'Why do you dress like a woman?' I don't dress like a woman. I dress like a drag queen. **99**

　　—*RuPaul*

HIDING HER CANDY

*D*on't go calling **The Lady Chablis** a drag queen. The "Grand Empress of Savannah" made famous by John Berendt in the bestselling *Midnight in the Garden of Good and Evil* doesn't like the label, because while she gets dolled up for performances, off stage she also lives as a woman. Chablis (formerly Benjamin Edward Knox) "sees herself simply as a person," according to a profile in *USA Today*, "born a man who grew up to be a woman" (sans sex change operation, although she has nothing against those who do go under the knife).

Hers is truly a drag to riches story. Born into poverty in Quincy, Florida, in 1957, she spent her early years with her aunt and grandmother and quickly came to see that the label "boy" just didn't fit. At age nine, she moved in with her mother and stepfather, who beat her for six years. She began cross dressing at age fourteen and ran away from home at age fifteen, assuming the name Chablis. During these years, she developed a drug habit, which she later kicked. She performed widely in Georgia in the late '70s and '80s with a strip show entitled "Lady Chablis and Her Men in Motion," but it wasn't until Berendt's book was published in 1994 that the former Miss Gay World hit the big time. *Oprah* and *Good Morning America* beckoned, crowds of tourists swarmed the club where she worked, and a big money (six figures) contract for her autobiography, *Hiding My Candy* (1996), as well as another six figures for the film rights, were forthcoming.

In addition to telling her life story, the book contains a number of recipes, the instructions for which reveal the lady's sassy style. Consider, for example her Kickin' Chicken: "First I rinse the chicken well. *Y'don't know if it ain't been whoring in the henhouse before it wound up in your grocer's freezer.* Then I pat it dry. *Pretend you're a dominatrix and give it a good swat!*"

True to her Southern roots, Chablis has strong connections to the women in her family—mother, grandmother, aunt. And while it hasn't always been easy for them, even her eighty-seven-year-old grandmother has learned to call her Chablis. Her other role models include Oprah Winfrey, Maya Angelou, and Whoopi Goldberg (although after seeing her in that purple and green gown Whoopi wore the first year she hosted the Oscars, Chablis proclaims, "Trust me, she does need some help on the wardrobe.") In 1987, she made her debut in black society by crashing the Alpha Phi Alpha Debutante Cotillion in Savannah and that same year she created the Savannah League of Uptown White Women, a group devoted to "Party, Talk and Alcohol." These days she plans to use her loot to open Chablis' Cabaret in Savannah's City Market to offer job security to the often low paid drag performers that have been her friends and mentors throughout the years.

66 It's a good thing that I was born a woman, or I'd have been a drag queen. **99**
   —Dolly Parton

90210H!

$\mathscr{A}$ctress **Shannen Doherty,** a Memphis native, has the reputation of a real tantrum thrower. Claiming that people think she's a bitch because they identify her with her former character, Brenda, on Fox's long running *Beverly Hills 90210*, (at one point there was even an "I Hate Brenda" newsletter), Shannen claims to be misunderstood. However, her involvement in a little literal "hit-and-run" incident with a woman at a bar, did nothing to enhance her reputation as a sweet innocent. Taking tips from Nellie Olsen instead of Half-pint, the former *Little House on the Prairie* star (her first role) was accused of belting a woman at a bar. Quickly turning the tables in true *Hell's Belles* style, she claimed that it was in fact, she who was hit, and not the other way around! Ultimately charges were dropped. She also claims she wasn't fired from the show, although media reports at the time spoke of tension with other cast members, chronic tardiness, being difficult to work with, and the disapproving glare of the show's producer Aaron Spelling, who felt Shannen was badly influencing his daughter, co-star Tori Spelling, several years younger than the tempestuous Shannen.

While starring in *Beverly Hills 90210*, she spent so much money she was eventually evicted from her $6,500 a month house and sued for $136,000 in damages to the house (the suit was settled privately in 1996). One of her spendthrift decisions was to buy a Porsche, even though she already had three cars, "because a friend said she should," reports *People.*

Fame and fortune came early and disappeared quickly for Shannen. She was only twenty-one when she hit it big on *90210*, and previously appeared in many television series, including *Little House on the Prairie*, NBC's *Our House*, and in teleflicks including one on a fellow belle called *Burning Passion: The Margaret Mitchell Story*, in which she played the great writer herself! While she has made a few theatrical films, including *Mall Rats,* and *Naked Gun 33 ⅓* in which she played herself, Shannen's career seems to have stalled on the highway of Hollywood.

Doherty is a popular subject on the Internet ("Did she have breast implants?" and "Where Can I see Shannen Doherty naked?" seem to be the main topics of so-called conversation. "Yes" and *"Playboy"* are the given answers). Her love life (including a bumpy romance with former brat-packer Judd Nelson) and a raucous, six-month marriage to model/actor Ashley Hamilton, the eighteen-year-old son of actor George Hamilton, seem to have met with the same fate as her career. And she is the first to admit it.

"I picked bad men. I picked men who were opportunists and were looking for press and looking for extra money." But her talent and ambition will certainly bring her back to the spotlight, and in the meantime, like any young belle in her prime, she needs to sow a few more wild oats, perhaps a little more privately this time.

❝I don't think anybody allowed me to grow up . . . Instead it was like this fleet of piranhas attacking me and putting me out there for a feeding frenzy.**❞**
    —Shannen Doherty

A Real Hell's Belle

*T*ruman Streckfus Persons, later known as the writer **Truman Capote,** was the original *enfant terrible.* The "tiny terror" was born in 1924 in New Orleans, but after his parents' divorce, was raised by his mother's relatives on a peanut farm in Monroeville, Alabama. A lonely, precocious, eccentric child, he spent his childhood writing, determined to become a famous author. He did have one friend in Monroeville—next door neighbor Harper Lee, known as Nelle, who went on to fame by penning *To Kill a Mockingbird* (although there were rumors in their hometown, when she won the Pulitzer Prize, that Truman wrote it for her). She would comfort the odd child who was always in trouble in school for knowing too much, "It's all right, Truman, that you know everything, even if the teachers don't understand." Later she would immortalize him as the character Dill in *To Kill a Mockingbird*: "His hair was snow white and stuck to his head like duck fluff . . . Beautiful thoughts floated around in his dreamy head. He could read two books to my one, but he preferred the magic of his own inventions." A dreamer, typical of the Southern genre of storyteller, Truman once claimed, in a not-so-far-fetched tale, to have tap-danced on a showboat as a child.

As a teen he went to live with his mother in New York City, but returned to Monroeville for vacations and even though he lived most of his life in the Big Apple, is considered a quintessential southern writer. At twenty-three, the southern gothic stylist vaulted to fame with his first novel, *Other Voices, Other Rooms.* Later he penned *Breakfast at Tiffany's,* a collection of short stories, many of which had first appeared in the *New Yorker,* and a novella that supplied the collection its title in which the diminutive dandy gave the world the hedonistic Holly Golightly (a.k.a. Lula Mae Barnes). But it was his Pulitzer-Prize winning reportage of the psychopathology of two killers,

In Cold Blood, that would provide his most lasting literary legacy.

Abandoned by his family as an adult because of his homosexuality, over time he became very vindictive: Cousin Jennings Faulk Carter claims in *A Bridge to Childhood*, "his memory was very long." Such vindictiveness came to the forefront when he published a portion of his forthcoming novel *Answered Prayers* (eventually to come to publication after his death) in *Esquire*, a *roman à clef* on the secrets and the dirty laundry aired among his socialite circle of friends. The cause for immediate banishment from their kingdom, Capote, formerly the royal jester, was thrown out of court, never to return.

Throughout his turbulent life, he remained supremely confident of his talent. When asked by an aunt about what he was going to write to follow up *In Cold Blood*, he said maybe nothing, despite having gotten a big contract for another book, boasting, "I've already written the world's best short story, 'A Christmas Memory,' and I've written one of the world's best books, *In Cold Blood*. They can wipe their behinds with those contracts, because now I've got plenty of money." It was a prophetic statement. After the enormous success of the "nonfiction novel" as he named it, he spent the next two decades cultivating the rich and famous and appearing on television talk shows and "working on" his much talked about *Answered Prayers*. When he died in 1984, it was still unfinished. In "Nocturnal Turnings," the witty, tragic talent wrote about himself, "I'm not a saint yet. I'm an alcoholic. I'm a drug addict. I'm homosexual. I'm a genius."

66 I don't care what anybody says about me as long as it isn't true. **99**

— *Truman Capote*

DIFFICULT?!

*B*orn Mary **Sean Young** in 1959 in Louisville, Kentucky, the actress famous for her role in the cult favorite *Blade Runner* first trained as a dancer at the school of American Ballet in New York. Because of her quirky way of handling things ("I look at my honesty as a virtue, but I really do have a high price to pay for it"), Sean Young developed a reputation as a "difficult" actor to work with, similar to her soul sister Shannen Doherty. It is a commonly-told tale that Sean stalked James Woods, her co-star in *The Boost*, culminating in the ominous leaving of a toy doll with its head ripped off on his front walk. She is also rumored to have shown up for an audition for the role of Catwoman in Tim Burton's movie *Batman Returns* dressed in full character, but lost the now famous part to a memorable feline Michelle Pfeiffer. Typical of the hot-one-minute-not-the-next world of Hollywood, she also has lost some of the lustre she once enjoyed as the bright new Hollywood star at the release of *No Way Out* with Kevin Costner in 1987. Recently making her professional stage debut in the Los Angeles production of *Stardust*, she seems to be fading, for now, into seeming obscurity. But perhaps she is only lying low, waiting to pounce back on the scene in a blaze of glory.

❝ I don't walk around thinking of myself as somebody who is difficult or somebody who is dangerous or somebody who is crazy. I don't perceive myself that way. That perception is floating around in some place that had almost no connection to me, except when other people give it energy, and that's about them. ❞

— *Sean Young*

"Dumb" (?) Belles
or
She Who Laughs Last

- **Vanna White,** of Myrtle Beach, South Carolina, who got rich off of looking good in a dress, keeping quiet, and knowing the alphabet. In 1997, after years of turning letters, Vanna leapt into the 21st century with a new, improved, and equally lucrative electronic letter board activated simply by the touch of a finger.

- **Marla Maples Trump,** from Dalton, Georgia (which bills itself as the carpet capital of the world), who unseated Ivana as first lady to "The Donald," was given the Miss Universe Pageant and access to a fabulous fortune the old fashioned way—by getting pregnant with little Tiffany.

- Former Miss Florida, **Delta Burke,** a.k.a. Suzanne Sugarbaker, the *Designing Woman* booted off the series for gaining weight and raising dander, now married to Gerald McRainey (*Major Dad*), dyed her hair blonde and launched her own line of clothes for "real-sized" women.

Out of the Mouths of Belles

❝Jimmy Carter as President is like Truman Capote marrying Dolly Parton. The job is just too big for him.**❞**

   —*Rich Little*

❝ College isn't the place to go for ideas.**❞**

   —*Helen Keller*

❝ If you want to say it with flowers, remember that a single rose screams in your face: 'I'm cheap!'**❞**

   —*Delta Burke*

❝ One day she was sitting on the porch and I said, 'Granny how old does a woman get before she don't want no more boyfriends?' (She was around 106 then.) She said, 'I don't know Honey. You have to ask someone older than me.'**❞**

   — *Jackie "Moms" Mabley*

ffRedneck women are the knot that will hold our culture together. We are far more complex and a lot stronger when we have men to hold together. Men would be nothing without us.™™

 —Jane, a self-described "proud redneck"

ffMy mother said it was simple to keep a man, you must be a maid in the living room, a cook in the kitchen, and a whore in the bedroom. I said I'd hire the other two and take care of the bedroom bit.™™

 —Jerry Hall

ffI have known the joy and pain of deep friendship. I have served and been served. I have made some good enemies for which I am not a bit sorry. I have loved unselfishly, and I have fondled hatred with the red-hot tongs of Hell. That's living.™™

 —Zora Neale Hurston

ffAmerican by birth, Southern by the Grace of God.™™

 —bumper sticker

ACKNOWLEDGMENTS

This book could not have been put together without the assistance of Jay Kahn; Mary Jane Ryan; Will Glennon; Ame Beanland; Jennifer Brontsema; Matthew Osborn; Suzanne Albertson; David Lauterborn of *Atlanta* magazine; Kimberly Andersen Cumber, Archivist for the North Carolina Department of Cultural Resources; Lee Eltroth, Archivist for the Georgia Women's Collections Project at Georgia State University; Ronald A. Lee, Reference Librarian for the Tennessee State Library and Archives; Lara Morris; Nina Lesowitz; Brenda Knight; Laura Marceau; Donald McIlraith; Claudia Schaab; Elise Cannon; Susan J. Paul; and all the Southern Belles on AOL. Special thanks to Roger Montoya.

BIBLIOGRAPHY

Gloria Adler, ed. *She Said, She Said: Strong Words from Strong-Minded Women*. New York: Avon, 1995.

Dorothy Allison. *Two or Three Things I Know for Sure*. New York: Dutton, 1996.

Maya Angelou. *I Know Why the Caged Bird Sings*. New York: Random House, 1969.

Maya Angelou. *Just Give Me a Cool Drink of Water 'fore I Die*. New York: Random House, 1971.

Ruth Ashby and Deborah Gore Ohrn, ed. *Herstory: Women Who Changed the World*. New York: Viking, 1995.

Regina Barreca, ed. *The Penguin Book of Women's Humor*. New York: Penguin, 1996.

John Berendt. *Midnight in the Garden of Good and Evil*. New York: Random House, 1994.

Joey Berlin. *Toxic Fame*. Detroit: Visible Ink Press, 1996.

Louise Bernikow. *The American Women's Almanac*. New York: Berkley Books, 1997.

Jean F. Blashfield. *Hellraisers, Heroines, and Holy Women*. New York: Superlative House, 1981.

Tanya Bolden. *The Book of African-American Women: 150 Crusaders, Orators, and Uplifters*. Holbrook, Massachusetts: Adams Media, 1996.

Rita Mae Brown. *Dolley*. New York: Bantam Books, 1994.

Holly Brubach, et. al. "Heroine Worship: A Special Issue." *New York Times Magazine*, November 24, 1996.

Bethany Bultman. *Redneck Heaven: Portrait of a Vanishing Culture*. New York: Bantam, 1996.

Truman Capote. *A Capote Reader*. New York: Random House, 1987.

Gerald Clark. *Capote*. New York: Ballantine Books, 1988.

Jennet Conant. "Married...with Buffalo." *Vanity Fair*, April 1997.

Pat Conroy. *The Lords of Discipline*. New York: Bantam, 1980.

Ernie Couch, comp. *Country Music Trivia & Fact Book*. Bethel, CT: Rutledege Hill Press, 1996.

Willard Delue. "The Death of Rebel Rose." *The State: Down Home in North Carolina*, January 14, 1956.

Earth Channel. "Brett Butler is On Target." *Best of The Comedy Magazine*, May/June, 1994.

Lois Stiles Edgerly, ed. *Women's Words, Women's Stories: An American Daybook*. Gardiner ME: Tilbury House, 1994.

Fannie Flagg. *Fannie Flagg's Original Whistle Stop Cafe Cookbook*. New York: Fawcett, 1993.

Gillian Gaar. *She's a Rebel*. Seattle, WA: Seal Press, 1992.

Trey Graham. "Lady Chablis Stays Sassy Well Past 'Midnight'." *USA Today*, December 2, 1996.

Darlene Clark Hine, et. al., ed. *Black Women in America: A Historical Encyclopedia*. Bloomington, IN: Indiana University Press, 1993.

Lisa Howorth. *Yellow Dogs, Hush Puppies & Bluetick Hounds: The Official Encyclopedia of Southern Culture Quiz Book*. Chapel Hill, NC: The University of North Carolina Press, 1996.

Insight Guides. *New Orleans.* Singapore: APA Publications (HK) LTD, 1994.

Molly Ivins. *Molly Ivins Can't Say That, Can She?* New York: Vintage, 1991.

Anne Janette Johnson. *Great Women in Sports.* Detroit: Visible Ink, 1996.

Neal T. Jones, ed. *A Book of Days for the Literary Year.* Thames and Hudson, 1984.

George Kalogerakis, et. al. "Red Alert." *People,* February 24, 1997.

Michael Kaplan. "Ashley Judd." *Us,* March, 1997.

Enrique Hank Lopez. *Conversations with Katherine Anne Porter.* Boston: Little, Brown, 1981.

Christine Lundardini. *What Every American Should Know about Women's History.* Holbrook, MA: Adams Media, 1997.

Loretta Lynn. *Loretta Lynn: Coal Miner's Daughter.* New York: Da Cap Press, 1996.

Axel Madsen. *Forbidden Lovers.* Secaucus, NJ: Citadel Stars/Carol Publishing, 1996.

Rosalie Maggio, ed. *The Beacon Book of Quotations by Women.* Boston: Beacon, 1992.

George Mair. *Oprah Winfrey: The Real Story.* Secaucus, NJ: Citadel Stars/Carol Publishing, 1996.

Barry McCloud. *Definitive Country: The Ultimate Encyclopedia of Country Music and Its Performers.* New York: Perigee, 1995.

Will N. Maxwell, ed. *The Country Music Guide to Life.* New York: Signet, 1994.

Nancy Milford. *Zelda: A Biography.* New York: Harper & Row, 1970.

Marianne Moates. *A Bridge of Childhood: Truman Capote's Southern Years.* New York: Henry Holt, 1989.

Sue Molyneaux, ed. *Pearl Fanzine Website for Janis Joplin.* http://www.ncf.cartlon.ca/~dg723/.

Eliot Nassour. *Honky Tonk Angel: The Intimate Story of Patsy Cline.* New York: St. Martin's Press, 1993.

Michael Newton. *Bad Girls Do It! An Encyclopedia of Female Murderers.* Port Townsend, Washington: Loompanics Unlimited, 1993.

Dan Parker. "Remembering Selena." *Caller-Times Interactive,* March 31, 1997. http://www.caller.com/newsearch/news3681.html.

Dolly Parton. *Dolly: My Life and Other Unfinished Business.* New York: HarperCollins, 1994.

Peter Pauper Press. *The Wit and Wisdom of Famous American Women.* White Plains, NY: Peter Pauper Press, 1986.

Pedro Pereira. "Martha Ingram." *Computer Reseller News,* November 18, 1996.

Dodson Radner. "There Had to Be Something More Out There." *Parade,* February 9, 1997.

Katherine Ramsland. *Prism of the Night: A Biography of Anne Rice.* New York: Penguin, 1991.

Barbara Reitt, ed. *Georgia Women: A Celebration.* Atlanta, GA: Atlanta Branch, American Association of University Women, 1976.

Darcy Rice. "Following her Bliss." *Orange Coast Magazine,* December, 1995.

Al Rose. *Storyville, New Orleans.* Tuscaloosa, AL: University of Alabama Press, 1974.

Bibliography

Phyllis Rose. *The Norton Book of Women's Lives*. New York: W.W. Norton & Co., 1993.

Sharon Malinowski and Christa Brelin. *The Gay & Lesbian Literary Companion*. Detroit: Visible Ink, 1995.

Marlene McCampbel "He Stopped Loving Her That Day." *Entertainment Weekly*, March 7, 1997.

Merriam-Webster Encyclopedia of Literature, New York: Prentice-Hall, 1995.

Karen Rosen. "Woman Trained on Albany Dirt Roads." *Atlanta Constitution*, 1995.

RuPaul. *Lettin' It All Hang Out!* New York: Hyperion, 1995.

The Selena Foundation. http.wwwneosoft.com/SELENA/selfound.html

Mr. Showbiz. *Star Bios*. http://www.mrshowbiz.com.

Carl Sifakis. *The Enclyclopedia of American Crime*. New York: Facts on File, 1982.

Jessie Carney Smith. *Epic Lives: One Hundred Black Women Who Made a Difference*. Detroit: Visible Ink, 1993.

Special Collections Library, Duke University. *Rose O'Neal Greenhow Papers: An On-line Archival Collection*. Duke University: specoll@mail.lib.duke.edu.

Maria St. Just. *Five O'Clock Angel: Letters of Tennessee Williams to Maria St. Just 1948-1982*. New York: Knopf, 1990.

Tamara Starr, ed. *Eve's Revenge: Saints, Sinners, and Stand-Up Sisters on the Ultimate Extinction of Men*. New York: Harcourt Brace, 1994.

Autumn Stephens. *Wild Women: Crusaders, Curmudgeons and Completely Corsetless Ladies in the Otherwise Virtuous Victorian Era*. Berkeley, CA: Conari Press, 1992.

_____ . *Wild Words from Wild Women*. Berkeley, CA: Conari Press, 1996.

_____ . *Wild Women in the White House: The Formidable Females Behind the Throne, On the Phone and (Sometimes) Under the Bed*. Berkeley, CA: Conari Press, 1996.

Brian F. Thomas, et al. "All the President's Women." *Beachbum's Clinton Scandal Page*. http://members.aol.com/beachbt/preswomn.htm

James Trager. *The Women's Chronology*. New York: Henry Holt, 1994.

Tina Turner. *I, Tina*. New York: Avon Books, 1986.

Andrew Vaughn. *Who's Who in New Country Music*. New York: St. Martin's Press, 1989.

Doris Weatherford. *American Women's History*. New York: Prentice Hall, 1994.

Eudora Welty *The Eye of the Story* New York: Vintage, 1979.

Wild Women Association. *Wild Women in the Kitchen: 101 Rambuctious Recipes and 99 Tasty Tales*. Berkeley, CA: Conari Press, 1996.

Charles Ragan Wilson and William Ferris, ed. *Encyclopedia of Southern Culture*. Chapel Hill, NC: The University of North Carolina, 1989.

INDEX

Index

Index

Index

Index

About the Author

Seale Ballenger is a native Alabamian (the cradle of the Confederacy) and 100 percent Southerner who has been temporarily stranded in a foreign land (California). Homesick and hungry for a good-humored dose of southern-fried fun (not to mention okra), the author cooked up this loving tribute to the women—the backbone of the South—who have raised hell, loved well and taken no guff while leaving their indelible, often magnolia-scented or Crisco-laden, but ultimately unforgettable, marks upon the world.

Wild Women Association

In 1992, with the publication of *Wild Women* by Autumn Stephens, Conari Press founded the Wild Women Association. Today there are over 3,000 card-carrying Wild Women in cities throughout the world—and some even meet regularly with their untamed and uproarious sisters in an effort to encourage wildness. The Association's primary purpose is to rediscover and rewrite our wild fore-sisters back into history. . . . and if there is a wild woman in your family we hope you might help by sending us information for possible inclusion in subsequent volumes of the "Wild and Ever-So-Uppity Women" series.

To become a member and to receive the Wild Women Association Newsletter, please mail this page to:

The Wild Women Association
2550 Ninth Street, Suite 101
Berkeley, CA 94710-2551

Let's rewrite history with women in it!

Conari Press, established in 1987, publishes books on topics ranging from spirituality and women's history to sexuality and personal growth. Our main goal is to publish quality books that will make a difference in people's lives—both how we feel about ourselves and how we relate to one another.

Our readers are our most important resource, and we value your input, suggestions, and ideas. For a complete catalog or to be added to our mailing list, please contact:

CONARI PRESS

2550 Ninth Street, Suite 101
Berkeley, California 94710-2551

Tel: 800-685-9595   Fax: 510-649-7190
E-mail: Conaripub@aol.com